so you want to be a wine merchant?

Joel Berman

So You Want to Be a Wine Merchant?

Published by Wheatmark®
2030 East Speedway Boulevard, Suite 106
Tucson, Arizona 85719 USA
www.wheatmark.com

ISBN: 978-1-62787-587-5 (paperback)
ISBN: 978-1-62787-588-2 (ebook)
LCCN: 2017961078

Contents

Contents

Some Additional Interesting Personages—245

Final Thoughts—257

Foreword

My Background

I have been a wine merchant for over fifty years. I started in 1962 working retail at my family business, Berman's Wine and Spirits in Lexington, Massachusetts. In 1961, in my junior year at Boston University, I enlisted in the army for a six-month tour of active duty, with five and a half years in the reserves. I ended my service with the rank of E-6 as a platoon sergeant in the 505th Military Intelligence Unit based in South Boston.

When I got out, at twenty-one years of age, I went back to BU nights and started work at the family business. Berman's was incorporated by my grandfather in 1909 and has had a liquor license since 1933. When my grandfather passed away in 1949, my dad and Uncle Ed inherited the business and were equal partners.

When I started working at our family's shop I knew nothing about business and less about wine. By working closely with my dad and uncle, I quickly grasped the nuances of our business and, ultimately, the reins. My dad stopped working a few years after I came on board, and my Uncle Ed soon did likewise. I was running Berman's at twenty-four years of age. Five years later, November 1972, I bought my uncle's shares of the business.

Wanting to become knowledgeable about wine, I went to weekly tastings and discussions with other wine professionals who were similarly inclined. I read everything I could find about wine and took diverse bottles home to try. After a period of time, I began to develop a certain level of wine sophistication. Back then there were no wine periodicals, like *Wine Advocate* or *Wine Spectator*, to guide or use as references. We learned largely by trying the wines ourselves or from invaluable word-of-mouth references from customers.

Although I was initially ignorant about wine I did have some excellent mentors. Foremost among them was Jack Stokes, who had a varied career in the wine business. He was part owner of a then avant-garde wine shop, S. Hooper Richardson, and he became import director for Dreyfus, Ashby & Company, then and now a large national import company. The first time Jack called on me and showed me some Bordeaux, he knew from my naïve questions that, as he put it, I "wasn't ready." Eventually we established a bond, and I went to his house for weekly tastings with other industry neophytes.

About this time, it must have been 1968 or 1969, I decided to expand the shop. I contracted a carpenter to start work in January, after the holidays. I had funds allocated for the work, but the carpenter never showed up. I then decided to invest that money in Bordeaux and ordered a number of cases of current-vintage Bordeaux: 1964 Ch. Beychevelle, 1964 Ch. La Lagune,1964 Ch. Pichon Baron, etc. I hadn't carried Bordeaux of this caliber before, so I priced them low, working on marginal percentages. To me, selling Bordeaux was like selling penny candy, just a "plus sale."

My wife, Bonnie, and I took off for our planned January vacation, and when we came back, to my amazement, many of the wines had completely sold out. When I called to order more Ch. Beychevelle I was told that the price was now sixty dollars a case.

"But I paid forty dollars two weeks ago," I said, perturbed.

"That was then, this is now," I was told.

That's when I knew I had to learn more about wine. For years Seagram's Seven was $55.65 for a case of quarts—that's right, quarts— and the price never varied. It was obvious to me that if one wasn't soon in the wine business, then one would soon be out of business.

At forty years of age, I decided to learn French, initially so that I could correctly pronounce French wine words like Pouilly-Fuissé (Poo YEE fweesay). It was one of the hardest things I have ever done. I began making twice-a-year pilgrimages to France with various importers, searching for wines worth buying. The ability to speak French directly to the growers was a huge advantage for me. However, after seeing some of my discoveries being imported successfully by others who had cleared (imported) the wines for me, I decided to become an importer myself. I started my import/distribution company, Arborway Imports, Inc., in 1989.

At the age of fifty, while at the annual wine fair Vinitaly in Verona, I felt lost because I spoke no Italian. I got by, but I wanted to speak directly to the growers to get the real scoop. When I got home, I called the Dante Alighieri Society to see if they had someone who could come to my home and teach me Italian. That started a twenty-plus-year relationship with Vincenzo Santone, who became my professor, mentor, and friend.

Introduction

Wine Is a Passion for Me

Wine is a love and passion for me. I feel fortunate, blessed really, that for over fifty years I have made my living dealing with fine wine. It has been a joy to enhance the wine-drinking pleasure of the many wonderful customers and clients that I have had over the years. I have been rewarded by their continued support and enthusiasm, and more than a few have become friends. I very well realize that while many people drink wine, only a small percentage actually care enough to seek out interesting nonmainstream offerings. Not many have the courage to take a chance on the unknown or unfamiliar. My job has been to broaden the horizons of those adventurous few and enlighten them along the way.

I think it's important to challenge customers by suggesting something unexpected or a food/wine pairing they may not have considered. I remember many years ago, a few days before Thanksgiving, a lady, probably in her fifties, came into my shop and asked me for a wine recommendation. I asked her how much she would like to spend. When she said "Around fifty dollars," I started to mentally come up with options. Finally, I said, "I have a dynamite wine here for forty dollars a bottle, but it's big and powerful. Does that sound good to you?" She said, "If you say it's good, then fine, I'll buy it," and she took two bottles. The wine I recommended was the Châteauneuf du Pape, Château Beaucastel. Obviously, this was quite a while ago, because Beaucastel now sells for over one hundred dollars a bottle. After she left I mentally kicked myself. I started to worry that maybe it was too much wine for her. Should I have given her something easier to drink for the holiday? I forgot about it until some months later when this same lady came into the shop and asked, "Do you remember me?" I thought to myself, "Uh oh. Am I in trouble?" She said, "You sold me two bottles of wine last Thanksgiving and told me they were 'dynamite.' Well, they were exactly that, and we loved them. Thank you!" That story just exemplifies why I love this business.

The Market and Trends Today

Unlike today, when I started out in the early '60s only an infinitesimal number of people cared about wine, fine or otherwise. For years we in the wine business kept waiting for the hoped-for "wine boom." When a wine boom finally did occur, it happened so subtly and stealthily that we were in it without even being aware of the change. A lot had to do with people traveling more extensively. They came back asking for, and expecting to find, favorites from their trip, such as rosés from Provence or pinot grigios from Italy.

There have been many positive changes in the wine and spirits business over the last half century. The craft-beer phenomenon has been explosive this past decade, and boutique "craft" bourbons and ryes as well as single-malt Scotches have also been flying off shelves. This demand for interesting, quality beverages positively impacts the fine wine industry too. Happily, wine quality has never been better. On these shores, rarely if ever will you find a poorly made wine. Boring or overpriced, yes, but rarely will we find an "undrinkable" wine.

Our job as wine merchants or sommeliers is to, unpedantically and without any trace of attitude, educate the interested wine-drinking public. We need to enlighten them to the myriad of options they have and the choices they can make. We should not just take the easy way out, the path of least resistance, when selling an interested party wine. There is a world of interesting, tasty, affordable wines that will enhance the dining experience. There is no need for compromise on choice, quality, or price.

I have noted a recent trend in the wine trade, especially in the restaurant business, where some young people have become less interested in traditional European wines, including Burgundies,

Rhônes, and Bordeaux. They call them, almost with a haughty touch of disdain, "classics" while they hunt for *vinous exotica.* They even call themselves "somms," not sommeliers. Change can be good. New things should be sought out, entrepreneurs encouraged, and innovative thinking embraced. However, there is a reason why wines considered classics have survived, advanced, and prevailed over the years. New trends may come and eventually may very well go. But the great wines of the world have weathered the test of time, have proven themselves, and will undoubtedly continue to be followed by those in the know.

Burgundy

Route Nationale 74

RN 74 is a busy two-lane highway that extends from the northern city of Dijon and meanders south, passing by the great Côte d'Or vineyards. It is one of the most renowned roads in the world. A famous Burgundy-friendly restaurant in San Francisco has even adopted RN 74 as their name. It passes by the great 1er Crus and Grands Crus vineyards of Vosne, Gevrey Chambertin, Chambolle Musigny, and Nuits Saints Georges in the Côte de Nuits. Then it traverses the great Côte de Beaune vineyards like Corton Charlemagne, Pommard, Volnay, Meursault, and Puligny-Montrachet. It ends further south in Chagny, home to the great three-star restaurant Lameloise, not far from the Mâconnais.

Much of my book deals with the wines and areas of Burgundy, both of which I unabashedly love and enjoy writing about. To be clear, I pretty much follow RN 74, the Route de Vin, when in Burgundy, starting in the north and then heading south to the Macon and Beaujolais areas, so that is how this book is set up. After Burgundy I head to the Rhône, often ending up very far to the south in the Languedoc. Then I head off to Italy. Of course, I occasionally have some side trips to Alsace and the Loire mixed in here as well. I hope you enjoy this ride along with me.

Thanks to the wine business I have traveled extensively to many parts of the world where grapes are grown. It sounds glamorous and exciting visiting seemingly exotic places, meeting interesting, highly intelligent people, and tasting great wine. While a lot of it is enjoyable, a tremendous amount of time, effort, and real work go into every trip, before, during, and after. The time spent in the field is precious, and the buying decisions are critical. There are no days off, Sundays included.

Once, when I was tasting in Meursault with grower Hubert Chavy-Chouet, he invited me to go fishing with him the next day, which was a Sunday. I begged off, explaining that I had appointments all lined up. He looked at me narrowly and, not believing a word of it, was quite obviously peeved. In fact, the next day I was headed to Macon and Beaujolais, where I was expected.

That Sunday, when in Fleurie, I made an unscheduled stop at a domaine that I had heard of but hadn't seen offered for sale in Massachusetts. I wanted to see if I could quickly try the current vintage to determine if we could do business and then continue on. After a few minutes, when no one answered the doorbell, I was set to leave. Just then an older gentleman came out to see what I wanted. I explained that I was an American importer interested in importing his wines and would like to taste them, if that was not inconvenient. "But of course," he said. "Let me just inform my wife. We are having a party celebrating our fiftieth wedding anniversary." What? "No, no sir," I said. "I don't wish to disturb you, your wife, or your guests. I can come back another time." "Non, monsieur," he said. "Don't worry about it. It's normal." Off he went to get a pipette and the key to the cellar. I felt sorry to have disturbed him, but he was quite correct: it was normal.

Over the years, many people have told me how lucky I am to be a wine merchant. I can't argue the point, but not all has been sweetness and light. There have been more than a few difficult moments, and more than a few that were downright comical. Here are a couple of examples.

Tasting in Burgundy with a Bigot

One cold February some years back, I was working with a noted Burgundy expert and longtime colleague visiting various growers, hoping to find some wine to buy. Last appointment in Gevrey Chambertin: my feet were ice cubes despite two pairs of socks and half-boots, bundled up but still cold in the grower's unheated, freezing cellar. I didn't know the man and had never tasted his wines, but I was aware of his wine reputation, which was solid. He looked to be in his early sixties, lean and tall, with a long, craggy, windburned face. When we were introduced he asked me in a guttural Bourguignon dialect, "Vous comprenez le Francais?" You understand French? I responded, "Oui, je comprend tout." Yes, I understand everything. We started the tasting with his Bourgogne Rouge. Nice, good fruit, priced fairly. We went on to some 1er Crus, then a couple of Grand Crus. We were smiling. Good juice, not overly expensive.

When courtiers and growers get together, they talk about lots of things, not all of them wine related. I was just waiting to get through with the day and go to dinner while they were both babbling on in rapid-fire French, I thought inconsequentially. Although my mind was elsewhere, I suddenly heard, out of nowhere, the grower loudly and angrily start disparaging various ethnic groups, including my own. That ended my reverie. My colleague/friend, the courtier, was horrified. He said to the man, "Arrêtez vous!" Stop! But the damage had been done! I just looked at the guy but said not a word. Anyway, what could I say to this bigot that might make any difference?

As we were heading for the car, I turned to my colleague and said, "Well, you almost made a sale." He looked at me, somewhat sheepishly, and said, "I understand, and I don't blame you."

Tasting at Dinner in Meursault

Another cold winter's night in Burgundy, after a day of nonstop tasting in icy cellars, my colleague and I dined at his rustic, unpretentious hotel located outside Meursault. We chose it not for the food but because they would allow us to bring in as many sample bottles to the dinner table as we could manage, and they would graciously provide us with spittoons. After a completely forgettable dinner, tasting eight or ten equally forgettable wines, suddenly looming over our table was a tall, fifty-ish, ruddy-faced, Ichabod Crane–like Englishman who was clearly perturbed.

We really hadn't taken any particular notice of anyone else at the sparsely attended restaurant, but as the man and his rather rotund wife were seated across the aisle from our table, I did notice them glancing our way periodically, I thought rather inquisitively. I guess I was wrong, as without preamble the English gentleman said, "Say, I want to let you fellows know that you were making a disgusting spectacle of yourselves, gurgling and spitting all that wine. My wife was repulsed."

It had been a long day. From the corner of my eye, I saw my colleague about to get up to confront the man. I put my hand on his arm, as if to say "Stop." Having not yet lost my sense of humor, I turned to the man and said, "Sir, we are very sorry if we offended you or your wife, but we are wine merchants and our time is precious. We need to work through dinner, trying various wines to see if they meet our quality and price standards; the restaurant knows this and accommodates us. But look, we have all these bottles on our table that we can't possibly finish. Please, allow me to present you with a few to take home, so as to make amends."

The man's face lit up as he turned to his wife and said, "Oh, Milly, these nice gentlemen are wine merchants, one from America! They were kind enough to offer us some wine to take home." She squealed appreciatively, and we gave them three or four bottles that were of no interest to us. They left beaming. Me, I wiped the sweat from my brow. Just another day at the office.

Burgundy Experiences

Every time I'm in Burgundy my heart beats a little faster. I am not a bit jaded after all these years! The old stone buildings found in the ancient townships of Meursault, Gevrey Chambertin, Vosne Romanée, etc. fill me with awe. The symmetrically placed vineyards of Puligny-Montrachet, Nuits Saint Georges, and Clos Vougeots among others, bursting with fruit in the fall, are spectacular. In late September the leaves begin to turn and resemble a patchwork quilt with ever-shifting colors that kaleidoscopically change daily. I love the variations that exist not only between wines from neighboring Burgundian villages, but also between adjacent or contiguous vineyards. Only a dirt road separates the world's most expensive piece of property, Romanée-Conti, from La Grand Rue, but, trust me, tasted blind you'd never confuse these two Grands Crus. Terroir is what separates them, not geography.

Terroir is defined by *Wine Spectator*'s Matt Kramer as a "sense of place." However, it includes more than the soil composition; it also includes the microclimate, drainage, mineral content, and a proprietary sense as well. That's why even DRC Richebourg tastes noticeably different than Romanée-Conti, even though there is just an invisible line separating the properties. If one were to try a bottle of Chambolle Musigny against wine from the adjoining village, Morey-Saint-Denis, or similarly, Nuits Saint Georges against Vosne Romanée, the discernable contrasts in the styles of these two side-by-side villages would be noticeable.

Red Burgundies are the most sensuous wines. At their best they are elegant and subtle, with finesse and delicacy. They can have an understated power even when almost translucent. They are not, nor should they ever be, excessively big or overly tannic. There is no wine from anywhere that can equal their flavor intensity, especially when married to fine food.

There are no other wines that engender the devotion shown by fans of Burgundy's great reds. There is a coterie of people who simply love Burgundy and who enjoy them exclusively, or drink other wines reluctantly. Many years ago, when I was mostly into Bordeaux, with only occasional forays into Burgundy, a middle-aged gentleman came into my shop. He looked around, picked up a couple of venerable Burgundy bottles, and then turned to me and said, "You know, I can only drink Burgundies now. Nothing else appeals to me." I probably looked at him as if he had two heads. I didn't understand him then, but I certainly get it now. If you were to tell me I could drink wine from only one region, Burgundy would be it.

Although there are some sumptuous pinot noirs now being

produced from vineyards around the world, especially from California and Oregon, I understand his preference for Burgundy. From Bourgogne Rouge to Chambertin, no other pinot noirs from anywhere taste quite like them, even those made in exactly the same manner by well-meaning, talented Frenchmen. Again, this is mostly due to that controversial French word, terroir. No wine can ever taste just like a Burgundy due to the unique Burgundian soil. It includes limestone and marlstone sub-soils, with silty clay/sandy topsoils that are enriched by various mineral deposits. The soil, through the root system, imparts the flavor, the so-called *gout de terroir*, the taste of the earth. And in no place else is it quite the same. This uniqueness is what captivates Burgundy lovers, and the fact that so little of it is produced. Often, in years where their crop size is cut nearly in half, like 2010 through 2013, three or four barrels are all that is available for the world. Sometimes it may even be just one lonely barrel, or less. There are twenty-five cases to a barrel. No wonder these great wines are not inexpensive.

I have often said/written that it is more important, when purchasing Burgundies, to know the producer (grower/vigneron) and vineyard site than just to focus on the vintage. For example, Clos Vougeots is separated into many individual parcels, with some seventy to eighty growers owning some part thereof. Some of the growers have excellent vineyard placement and work the fields strenuously to grow quality grapes. Others are equally well situated but have, shall we say, a less intense work ethic and are profligate with their natural resources. Others have less-good plots but work assiduously to honor the land by making wine worthy of the Grand Cru appellation. All are labeled "Clos Vougeots," so how does one know which producer to choose or, more importantly, which to avoid?

Generally speaking, an established, quality-oriented grower/vigneron can make better wine in a medium vintage than a sloppy, less competent grower can in a very good year. And Premier Cru and Grand Cru vineyards, with midslope exposure, can, even in not-great years, avoid the problems of *villages* wines, which are usually located down in the flats and have poorer drainage. Burgundies can be challenging, for professionals and *amateurs de vin* alike. That's one of the reasons I go there so often.

Surprises

There can often be some unexpected, not always happy, surprises when it comes to Burgundy. I can remember tasting the 1990 Clos Vougeot in cask at Domaine Rene Engel in Vosne Romanée with Paris-based Burgundy expert Peter Vezan, with whom I have worked for years. Tasting the new vintage in cask, before bottling, can give a good indication of what the wine will be like, qualitatively, some years later. After bottling, the wines close down and take time to get over their confinement in glass. This Clos Vougeot from a great red Burgundy vintage was magnificent. Unusually dark, almost black, and heavily concentrated, the wine was full on the palate, with deep, sappy flavors of dark red currents, earth, and a hint of smoke. The wine was joyous and compelling, not at all austere, as are many young Clos Vougeots. Of course, Engel's Clos Vougeot vineyard was located not far from his Grands Echezaux vineyard, and the two wines had much in common.

I enjoyed tasting with Philippe Engel as he was always enthusiastic, with an exuberant personality. He was maybe five feet eight inches tall and just a little bit chubby. Philippe, who was a lifelong bachelor, was a fun guy who liked to have a good time. I once made the mistake of taking my daughter, Erica, to taste there with me. Philippe was entranced by her and tried wooing her while we tasted. He had not a chance, as she was going with someone at the time, but I gave him an "A" for effort and found the interaction between them amusing.

Once Engel had bottled his 1990s, Vezan and I went back to try the wines. We went with much anticipation and high expectations, especially for Engel's Clos Vougeot, as we well remembered how great it was in cask. Imagine our shock and disappointment when the wine in bottle, while still great, lacked that extra dimension of depth, concentration, and character it had when tasted from the barrel. We looked at each other in amazement and regarded Philippe quizzically. Finally we asked him what he had done to his wine. We wanted to know why it didn't have the same concentration that it had from the barrel. Philippe shrugged his shoulders and said, "I did what I always do. Nothing has changed." We persisted, and finally Philippe admitted that maybe he filtered just a bit more than he should have in such a great vintage. We groaned inwardly and gently asked, "Why would you do that? The wine was fabulous as it was." Of course, Philippe's stock response was that he was afraid of any possible sediment or deposit in his wine. The clients, restaurateurs, and importers alike would either send the wine back or never buy from him again. We just shook our heads and lamented. While no one but those who had tasted it in cask would ever know the difference, a monumental wine was missed. It was still a great Clos Vougeot, but we knew what it could have been, and that was too bad.

Unfortunately, on May 23, 2005, Philippe had a heart attack and passed away while on vacation in Tahiti. After Philippe's death, the domaine was sold for mega bucks to the owners of Château Latour. The Engel Domaine is now called Domaine d' Eugénie, and the wines are purportedly even better than they were, which is saying a lot. But they are *far* more expensive, as could be expected.

There are occasional happy surprises. Neither the colleague I was traveling with nor I had ever been particularly enamored with wines from François Lamarche's La Grand Rue vineyard. They should have been great, but sadly, most often they were not. The wine comes from a Grand Cru vineyard located between La Tâche, Romanée-Saint-Vivant, La Romanée-Conti, and La Romanée, with only a dirt road separating them. It had been an underachiever for years, despite the fabulous vineyard placement. On one of my trips, while dining at a restaurant we often frequented, and whose owner knew us well, we tried, on his recommendation, the latest vintage of La Grand Rue. The price he was extending to us couldn't be refused. Still, we had no great hope for a stellar experience. When the wine came and we tried it, we were once again amazed, but this time positively. The wine was full of life, deep, dark, rich, and full of flavor. It was truly a

Grand Cru worthy of its appellation. Smiling broadly, my companion turned to me and memorably said, "Joel, this wine is like two homely people who just, astonishingly, gave birth to the most beautiful baby on earth."

Domaine Hudelot-Noëllat

Unfortunately, when Philippe Engel passed away there was no successor and no provision for one. His brother, Frédéric, wasn't interested in doing the work, and his mother was too old to even think about what needed to be done. The subsequent sale of the Domaine Rene Engel vineyards to François Pinault, owner of the Château Latour, caused concern and consternation in Burgundy. The Burgundians were upset to learn that "the Bordelais" had swooped in and scooped up the justly famous Engel vineyards, even though they paid an astronomical thirteen million euros for it. They were even less happy when insult was added to injury by the renaming of the domaine after François Pinault's grandmother, Eugénie. They were apoplectic and could talk of nothing else for weeks. None of which did me any good. The new owners were never going to sell to me, although I tried. I now needed to find another Burgundy domaine that had top-notch 1er Crus and Grands Crus. One of my colleagues in the South of France with whom I do business recommended that I try Alain Hudelot in Vosne Romanée.

I did some research and learned that Domaine Hudelot-Noël-lat is one of the premier estates in Burgundy. Based in Chambolle Musigny since the early 1900s, they have some of the most exten-sive and prestigious vineyard holdings one could dream about: Richebourg, Romanée-Saint-Vivant, Clos Vougeots, three different Vosne Romanée 1er Crus, Chambolle Musigny les Charmes, Nuits Saint Georges Les Murgers, and more. They all get extensive praise and high points from every wine writer who has tried them. So, needless to say, I was psyched but a little apprehensive about going there.

Alain Hudelot, who was born in 1940, is a large man with a florid, open, craggy face and dark eyes that exude good nature and intelligence. When I was first introduced to him and he learned that I was American, refreshingly, to my immense relief, he gave a great big smile. It turns out that he loves America and Americans. He lived through WWII and its privations and appreciates America's sacrifice and effort to liberate France. He was quite vocal about it.

Alain showed me his cave (cellar) and the extensive, impressive amount of lovely 2005s resting in barrels, contentedly aging. Most were going through malo (malolactic fermentation) so I couldn't taste them then, but wished I could. Instead, he asked me what I would like to taste that was already in bottle. Hmm. I said, "How about a bottle of 2004 Chambolle Musigny 1er Cru Charmes and a bottle of 2003 Romanée-Saint-Vivant?" He agreed and went off to fetch the bottles. My request had been rather reflexive, and once I thought about it, while he was gone, I began to rethink myself.

When M. Hudelot came back with the bottles. I asked him, because I hadn't done so before, "How much are these wines?" When he told me the price of the Romanée-Saint-Vivant, a bottle that would retail for $400-plus a bottle then and more than double that today, I said, "That is very kind of you, sir, but I cannot ask you to open a wine that expensive just for me to taste." He looked me quizzically and appraisingly for a bit and then handed me the bottle. "In that case," he said, "You take it home and try it there." You can be sure that I did.

I bought some cases of his 2004s, including the Romanée–Saint-Vivant. This was one of the worst vintages of the past decade in Burgundy, but his wines were good. That cemented a long-lasting, mutually beneficial relationship. I daresay it is more beneficial to me than to him, as he could sell his fabulous Burgundies in a heartbeat to any number of people. And, yes, I did get a very fair allocation of those scrumptious 2005s.

Alain Hudelot began buying up high-quality vineyard sites approximately fifty years ago, including part of his own father's holdings in Clos Vougeot. In 1963 he married the granddaughter of

Charles Noëllat, despite the inexplicable vehement opposition of her family. Married people all have to deal with in-laws. She married him anyway, despite their threat to cut her out of her dowry, a precious few rows of 1er Cru vines. Nice.

From 2008 on, Alain's sharp and very nice grandson, Charles Van Canneyt, has increasingly dealt with the multiple tasks required at the domaine. Talented winemaker Vincent Mugnier has been there since 2005.

I love the style of the wines produced at Hudelot-Noëllat. They are expressive, fresh, and stylish and show the requisite elegance and finesse, with understated power and subtlety that is found only in top-of-the-line Burgundy. They have that ineffable, impossible-to-duplicate, velvety style that only pinot noir produced from the *great* Côte de Nuits vineyards can display. Bottom to top, from Bourgogne Rouge to Richebourg and back again, they all display the Hudelot pedigree! My mouth is watering just thinking about them.

Since I love the Burgundy region and its glorious wines, I have made multiple visits there over the years. This has resulted in some memorable occurrences, which I am now about to share with you. Some are amusing; some were less so to me at the time.

I have had interesting episodes in every place I have visited over the years. I will include some of these in their proper place, when I get to the section dealing with their respective areas. I hope that you, gentle reader, find them to be enjoyable, if not enlightening.

Visiting Domaine Ponsot

What I love most about Burgundy, aside from the incomparable, glorious wine, is that the area remains, for the most part, unchanged and unspoiled. The vineyards remain as they were decades if not centuries ago. They, and the stone walls and buildings in their various villages, are as they have been since I began going there thirty-plus years ago. They are, to me, as beautiful, enchanting, and endlessly fascinating as they were the first time I saw them. They still evoke wonder, awe, and reverence in me.

When working in Burgundy, I almost always stay in the village of Puligny, just south of Meursault. I used to stay at the Inn, Le Montrachet, which is better than ever since it was renovated four to five years ago. The expansion and renovation kept to the original design and décor, with extra work done beautifying and enlarging the dining room and bar area. The food is better than ever too.

However, I now stay diagonally across the street at La Chouette, a newer, charming, far smaller B and B owned by Suzanne and Thierry, who have run, and still run, le Montrachet for well over twenty years. From Puligny it is easy for me to visit any of the growers with whom I do business. To get to the Côtes de Nuits, I usually pass through the also unsullied, charming city of Beaune by circling the ring road (*périphérique*), unless I decide to take the *autoroute* (highway) to Nuits Saint George. I prefer to go through Beaune when not in a hurry.

In May of 1988 my wife, Bonnie, accompanied me on one of my buying trips to Burgundy. She came with me very infrequently, because even though we would work a much shorter day than ordinarily, with fewer visits, it still was arduous. Most growers/vignerons expect you to taste their entire gamut of offerings, often more than a dozen wines, and older vintages of many of the same as well. I am usually happy to do so, depending on the grower, as I want to learn as much as I can, but Bonnie was just along for the ride.

As this was in mid-May, the weather was warm and lovely, in the midseventies. On this fine day, we were off to visit Domaine Ponsot, owners of legendary vineyards in the Côte d'Or. When we arrived at the domaine, located at the top of the village of Morey St. Denis, up the Rue du Montagne, we were greeted not by Laurent Ponsot, whom we had expected to see, but his father, Jean-Marie, who explained that Laurent had been in a very bad automobile accident and was in the hospital.

M. Ponsot, who appeared to be in his late fifties or early sixties, was rather tall for a Burgundian. He was maybe a six-footer, burly and strong-looking as well. As we descended into his deep, dark cave, I was glad we had taken warm coats. It was no more than 40° Fahrenheit down there, if I were to give a guess, in stark contrast to the almost balmy weather outside. Surprisingly, M. Ponsot was only wearing a t-shirt. Bonnie turned to me and said, "This gentleman must be in great shape, if that's all he needs to wear." M. Ponsot heard her comment, but, as he didn't speak any English, asked me, "Qu'est-ce qu'elle a dit?" What did she say? I explained that Bonnie had said that he looked to be in great shape. He smiled broadly and said, "Moi, je suis en grande forme." I *am* in great shape.

After that the ice was broken, and he shed any lingering reserve. He then gave us a memorable tasting of his magnificent Burgundies with a highly educational running commentary on each wine. We were tasting his 1987s, a vintage not unlike the 2001s, 2006s, and 2011s of today. The 1987 vintage, like those three vintages, was not construed as being "great," but what they all have in common is beautiful transparency and crystalline clarity, and they clearly show the individual characteristics of each vineyard site. There is far better, more enlightened winemaking going on today than was the case back then, but the Ponsot wines from their exalted, legendary vineyard sites were fabulous. Included were the incomparable Grands Crus of Clos de la Roche Vieilles Vignes, Clos Saint Denis, Griottes Chambertin, Chapelle Chambertin, Chambertin Clos de Beze, Chambertin, and Clos Vougeots. There were villages wines and 1er Crus from Morey-Saint-Denis and Chambolle Musigny to sample as well. It was almost a pity to have to spit out these gorgeous wines, but we would have never made it through the afternoon, or out of his cellar, if we didn't. I can taste that Griotte Chambertin still.

He opened a few older wines for us as well. The one wine I remember the most vividly was his 1976 Clos de la Roche Vieilles Vignes. Like 2003, 1976 was an abnormally hot vintage in Burgundy, and this wine was thicker and more concentrated than usual. It was still black in color, thick, almost Rhône-like in weight and size, with obvious old-vine sap and power. The firm, well-structured flavors were intense and earthy with red-current overtones, but that really doesn't do the wine justice. This was an original, "old-school"

Burgundy that even back then was unique. We certainly don't find wines like that today, even from Ponsot.

Before leaving, M. Ponsot turned to me and asked, "Est-ce que vous avez de la patience?" Do you have patience, or are you a patient person? I said, "Sure, I think so." He went and got a dust-covered bottle of the same 1976 Clos de la Roche VV that we had just tasted and said, "Then take this, and don't drink it too soon." You can be sure I carted it home with me and let it rest for a long, long time before pulling the cork. Yes, thanks to Bonnie, we did hit it off quite well.

By the way, Laurent thankfully did survive that horrendous automobile accident, but he was so badly injured that he no longer was able to work the fields. Of course, he had plenty to keep him occupied running the domaine and overseeing operations. Laurent may be best known to the international wine world not as much for his great Ponsot wines that collectors fight to purchase, but for being the man who uncovered a scandal involving counterfeit bottles of his wine. A wine collector named Rudy Kurniawan consigned several vintages of Ponsot wine to the New York auction house of Acker, Merrall & Condit. These included Clos St. Denis 1945, 1949, 1959, 1962, 1966, and 1971, and a 1929 Clos de la Roche. Interestingly enough, the domaine only began to estate bottle after 1934. And they never made any Clos St. Denis prior to 1982.

Laurent Ponsot somehow got wind of this lot and was mystified and suspicious. He contacted auction officials about his concerns and came to the States to see for himself. After the auction lots were pulled, Laurent wondered if Kurniawan was "a victim or predator," but once he met with Kurniawan, he became convinced that "it was the latter." He ascertained that there was no way those bottles could have been authentic and, upon inspection, he found label and corking inconsistencies as well. This was no small matter, as the bogus wines were valued at over $600,000. After that point, he began working with the FBI in the matter of the faked wines. Ultimately, the collector who submitted the fraudulent wine, Rudy Kurniawan, was tried and convicted in federal court and was sentenced to ten years in prison. Laurent Ponsot testified for the prosecution.

Gros Family Domaines: Is This a Dynasty?

The village of Vosne Romanée contains fifteen 1er Crus and six of Burgundy's greatest Grands Crus, including Romanée Conti and La Tâche. The Gros family name in Vosne Romanée, which dates back to the beginning of the nineteenth century, is one of the most famous in all of Burgundy. However, as there are now four separate Gros domaines, it is often one that causes the most confusion. Here's the deal: in 1996 Jean and Jeanine Gros, owners of Domaine Jean Gros, retired and divided the domaine between their three children: Michel, Bernard, and Anne-Françoise. There is **Domaine Michel Gros** in Vosne Romanée, **Domaine Gros Frère & Soeur** run by Bernard in Vosne Romanée, and **Domaine Anne-Françoise Gros** in Pommard. Each domaine is run completely separately, and each is totally autonomous.

Domaine Anne Gros, also based in Vosne Romanée, is owned by, you guessed it, Anne Gros. She is the cousin of Michel, Bernard, and Anne-Françoise, as Anne's father, François, was Jean's brother. Much of the four Gros' Vosne Romanée properties are contiguous, and all offer high-quality Burgundies. There are discernible differences between their wines, but much similarity exists despite somewhat differing winemaking philosophies. They all make a small amount of the fabulous, very hard-to-procure Grand Cru Richebourg, which from any one of them would be great.

I used to do business with Domaine Jean Gros prior to Jean and Jeanine's retirement, before they divided it up. I have fond memories of the not young, very stately, elegant, but always warm Jeanine Gros, hair pulled back severely in a bun, who invariably conducted our tastings in Vosne. Their Vosne Romanée 1er Cru Clos des Reas was always one of my favorites.

Domaine Gros Frère & Soeur

For the past several years I have been doing business with Bernard Gros, owner of Domaine Gros Frère & Soeur. I visited Bernard Gros in March of 2014 and was again very impressed with the size and beauty of the domaine. Bernard is not like most Bourguignon vignerons, who wear old jeans, faded work shirts, and functional, unstylish jackets. Not Bernard, at least not when I was there. When I last saw him, he was nattily dressed in a white shirt, contemporary sports jacket, dress pants, and loafers. He was eloquent about his wines and the domaine and was surprisingly erudite. It was a beautiful sunny day when he was conducting the tasting, and he must have been in an expansive mood. After trying his lovely 2013s in cask, we went back upstairs, and Bernard went to his grand piano and started playing and singing for us. Unprecedented, this was most definitely a first for me in Burgundy. He was really good, very talented, and we all had a great time. We loved his wines, which were very aromatic, easy to like, and stylish. He makes a lovely Hautes Côte de Nuit Rouge. A standout is his Clos Vougeot Musigni, which is so named for its proximity to Musigny vineyards. Lovely wine.

Domaine Anne Gros

The first vintage I bought from Anne was her 1989 vintage, made when she was not yet twenty years old and unproven. She took over for her dad, François, in 1988, when he became ill and was unable to work. She was eighteen years old at the time. It boggles my mind to think of a twenty-year-old girl in chauvinistic Burgundy taking over sole responsibility of such a prestigious domaine, even if she had been around the vineyards in Vosne all her life. She, of all the members of the Gros family, has earned the greatest renown for her wines with a loyal international following. There is no way she could ever completely satisfy the wide demand for her wines. If I hadn't gotten in on the ground floor, grandfathered in, so to speak, there is no way I could ever get to represent her wines today.

Anne Gros is not an ordinary woman—not then and not now. She not only took over the domaine, she improved everything about the operation. Although things had slipped a bit, due to her dad's ill health, she put things right and then some. At twenty-five years of age, Anne more than doubled the family domaine from three to six and a half hectares. Having known Anne almost from the beginning, I have seen her grow and develop. As you might imagine, Anne is a highly intelligent, extremely strong-willed, focused, almost driven person who is passionate about her craft. The French would call her *formidable!* She suffers fools not at all. Her time is far too valuable to waste.

Tasting with her is invariably in her immaculate cave. Unlike most other growers with whom I have worked, she is quick and efficient, doling out small tastes from her pipette, which she daintily dips into various casks while commenting on the wines and the vintage. There is most certainly no spitting on these floors. She pushes a wheeled *crachois* (spittoon) from barrel to barrel for us to spit into. There is no wasted wine either. Take a taste, pour the rest back in the barrel. This is liquid gold; not a drop is to be lost. We are not offered any old vintages to try (drink) here.

Anne maintains that the secret to her success is not exactly simple. She says, "The goal of the game is to obtain ripe and healthy grapes. I then strive to bring everything together while respecting the integrity of our grapes. This philosophy is in keeping with a respect for tradition and a desire to innovate. Respecting the biodiversity of the terroir allows us to produce wines that are subtle, harmonious, and elegant, with good stuffing, viscosity, and fruit."

Although I have known Anne and have tasted at the domaine many times over the years, we never have had what I would call a warm relationship. Cordial, yes, but she is all business. I learned early on that the best course of action with Anne is to say very little, nod approvingly about the wines, not hard to do, and not rock the boat. Some years back, she decided to modernize her labels. The ones she traditionally used were rather elegant, old-style Burgundy labels. I liked them, a lot. The new labels didn't look very "Burgundian" to me, but when she asked me how I liked them, I knew I had to say that they were very nice. Her mind was made up and they were printed anyway, so that was just a formality.

One time I made the mistake of saying I thought that her 1995 Bourgogne Rouge was the best she had ever made. "Cà, c'est le meilleur Bourgogne Rouge que vous ayez jamais faites." She just looked at me and said, "What was wrong with the others?" Uh oh. Another time we were just conversing in general, and in response to something we were talking about I said, "La vie est compliqué." Life is complicated. She turned to me and said, "Non, Monsieur Berman, la vie n'est pas compliqué." Really, I thought. Life is not complicated? You are running one of the most prestigious Burgundy domaines while raising three kids and taking care of a husband. The myriad decisions necessary to take care of the vineyards and vinify the wine are beyond my calculations, forget the kids. But to her, seemingly, life is not complicated. I don't get it. So when I go there, I smile a lot, nod my approval, and try not to say too much.

Maison Remoissenet
Père et Fils/Pierre-Antoine Rovani

Some years ago, one of my good Burgundy-loving customers went on a guided tour of some of the great Grand Cru–producing Burgundy estates: Domaine Comte de Vogüé, Domaine de la Romanée Conti, Domaine Roumier, Jean Grivot, and others. He came back raving about the wines at Maison Remoissenet even in that context and implored me to get on a plane and go see them. Timing is everything in life and, as luck would have it, I was scheduled to leave for Burgundy two weeks later. I called my colleague, Burgundy expert Peter Vezan, to see if the wines really were that good, and Peter said, "By all means go. The wines are on another level from those that were made under Roland Remoissenet now that

Pierre Rovani is in charge." I wasted no time making an appointment to go there to taste and meet with Rovani.

I did a bit of research before going and learned that Remoissenet Père et Fils was founded in 1877. It was a *négociant* firm like Louis Jadot, Albert Bichot, Joseph Drouhin, and Louis Latour. Like them, they also owned several parcels of excellent vineyard sites ranging from Bourgogne Rouge to Grands Crus like Charmes Chambertin and Clos Vougeots. For thirty years it was run by Roland Remoissenet, now in his eighties, with varying degrees of success, but, frankly, I was never a fan. Roland did have a huge cache of older cru wines to sell, but I was never tempted to offer any. I was always leery of them. I don't like hit or miss, and I wouldn't gamble on them at the prices asked. In 2005 Roland decided to retire and sold the company to neophyte Burgundy lovers and New York financiers Eddie and Howard Milstein.

Enter Pierre-Antoine Rovani. Born in 1964 in Washington, DC, Pierre graduated from Vanderbilt University. Before working at *The Wine Advocate*, Pierre worked on Capitol Hill and helped write some laws. The multitalented Rovani was a White House correspondent and a business consultant who, with a partner, also founded an electronic publishing company. Then his passion for wine won out and he became a wine merchant, buying and selling wines for Andy Bassin, owner of the highly regarded MacArthur's Beverages in Washington, DC. Thereafter Pierre worked for ten years with Robert Parker at *The Wine Advocate*, writing reviews. He covered many regions, mostly in France, but he was most noted for his evaluations and writings on Burgundy. The Millsteins were brilliant to have hired Pierre Rovani as president, as he has transformed the entire Remoissenet domaine. Also brought on board was the colorful Bernard "Bernie" Repolt, formerly president of Maison Louis Jadot, as director general. Claudie Jobard, a highly intelligent, dynamic young woman, was installed as winemaker.

I had never met Pierre previously but had, of course, read and admired his writings in *The Wine Advocate*. I felt a bit starstruck meeting him for the first time, as if he were a movie star or famous athlete, but Peter Vezan assured me that he was a "good guy." Peter was nice enough to accompany me to the vast Remoissenet holdings on the outskirts of Beaune for the meeting or I might still be looking for it. It was a freezing cold November evening, but Pierre was warm and welcoming. Peter left us, as he had a previous appointment.

Pierre is a larger-than-life fellow. He is big, over six feet tall, and heavy but handles it well and is light on his feet. He has a large, round face with lots of laugh lines. His large brown eyes brim with intelligence, and it is obvious from the moment he begins speaking, this is a person of high intellect—but not a snob. He is down-to-earth, witty, perceptive, and sharp. Obviously, he is nobody's fool. We went through the entire gamut of Remoissent wines starting with Bourgogne Blanc and Bourgogne Rouge, then, happily, ended up with Bonnes Mares, Charmes Chambertin, and their ethereal Le Montrachet from the fabulous Baron Thénard Estate. I was more than convinced of the quality and placed an immediate order. I silently sent a word of thanks to my friend who had suggested I go there.

Pierre has increased the Remoissenet holdings by adding more crus and has solidified relationships with growers by having invaluable contracts that were so necessary during the four years of penury: 2010, 2011, 2012, 2013.

Pierre and I almost immediately became fast friends, and I feel privileged to have known him and to have worked with him and his Remoissenet wines for the past several years.

Robert Arnoux—A Friend

I was told by various courtiers representing Burgundian vignerons that the odds of my befriending, or being befriended by, a Burgundian winemaker would be small to nonexistent. "Burgundians are insular, suspicious, close-minded, and stubborn. They won't even go to the neighboring villages," they said. Robert Arnoux wasn't like that and, despite our considerable differences, not least of which was size, we became surprisingly friendly over the years. Robert Arnoux, at six feet seven inches tall, was an anomaly in Burgundy thirty years ago.

Even today, a man of that height would be quite rare. I enjoy the fact that most Burgundians with whom I work are more my size, a foot shorter than that. Robert had one of the most pronounced Bourguignon accents that I had ever heard. I mentioned this to François Faiveley one day while tasting with him, and he started laughing. He told me that his wife, Anne, who was English, had François translate for her when conversing with Robert, as she couldn't understand a word he said.

Robert Arnoux passed away unexpectedly in 1995. Legend has it that while he was visiting a friend in the hospital he was stricken with a heart attack, and nothing could be done to save him. He left his wife and four daughters. Since his passing, Domaine Robert Arnoux has been run by Robert's son-in-law, Pascal Lachaux, with the domaine still right on RN 74 in Vosne Romanée, on the border of Nuits Saint Georges. Since 2007 the wines are all labeled Arnoux-Lachaux. The domaine has a superstar lineup of 1ers Crus and Grands Crus, all with excellent vineyard placements, and most with very old vines. They include Bourgogne Rouge produced from sixty old vines, village wines from Nuits Saint Georges and Vosne Romanee, superb 1er Crus from these villages as well. Those wines and their monumental Grands Crus from Clos Vougeots, Echezaux, Latricieres Chambertin, and Romanée Saint-Vivant are routinely tasted, usually several vintages worth, when at their cave. This takes a lot of time and allows one to know the style of the wines and the grower.

After conducting an extensive tasting, Robert would fetch an older vintage bottle of one of the wines we had just tried, as he liked us to try to guess the vineyard site and the vintage. As the wines remained *déshabillé* (undressed) or unlabeled, we never knew what he was offering us. I can't say that I was overly successful at these exercises but I had my moments. I do remember one distinctly. It must have been 1989 or 1990. Robert came back with a cobwebbed, dust-covered bottle and grinned as he poured a bit out for us. I do, fortunately, have good palate memory and, while the wine was definitely not young, it did resemble fairly closely one of the wines we had previously tried. By the color and aroma I deduced that it was a

1983 and, by the flavor, Clos Vougeots. When I told him I thought it was his 1983 Clos Vougeots, he broke out in a great big smile. I nailed it, and we were, though perhaps not quite buddies, very warm acquaintances from then on.

When I made the hard decision to strike out and begin my own wholesale operation, I talked about it with Robert. I explained that I was less concerned with succeeding than with hurting some of the kind folks who used to take me on trips to visit growers like him. Sure, they had an ulterior motive to sell me lots of wine, which they did, but I felt a bit guilty, as they not only would lose my business, but I would be actively competing with them as well. Robert listened to me and finally said, "Look. We in Burgundy have all these adjoining villages like Vosne Romanée and Nuits Saint Georges, Morey-Saint-Denis and Chambolle Musigny. We all compete, sometimes fiercely, but at the end of the day, we all get along. I wouldn't worry about it if I were you." Strangely enough, that advice comforted me, and when I did inform various suppliers of my decision prior to starting my company, nearly all were supportive and thankful that I had given them a heads up.

The Greatest White Burgundy Producer? Domaine Comtes Lafon

Dominique Lafon took over management of the prestigious Domaine Comtes Lafon from his father in 1984, but I knew him prior to that when he worked for a short time as a salesman for M. S. Walker Company in Boston. Dominique, in his midtwenties then, was an excellent salesperson. He was a nice, personable young man who had no airs about him. He was not an expert wine salesman, nor was he considered a Burgundy specialist. We saw him as just another young man trying to get by while learning the wine business. He was always anxious to please.

Fast forward to today, and Dominique is one of the most respected, powerful people in Burgundy, and that is saying a lot.

Domaine des Comtes Lafon is considered one of the finest, most efficiently run Burgundy domaines. Less than a handful of Burgundy producers can be mentioned in the same breath as this magical estate. Under the direction of Dominique, Comtes Lafon makes an array of sumptuous Meursaults, a small amount of Grand Cru le Montrachet, and some delicious 1er Cru Volnays. Their limited-production Burgundies are among the most sought after by those in the know, almost always to no avail. They are among the hardest to procure of any of the great Burgundy domaines.

Dominique is as protective of his wines as he is imperiously intelligent, and he is highly intelligent. He circumvents even gray market sales of his wines by using an intricate numbering system on his cases. Any Lafon customer caught selling gray market, be it Parisian restaurant or major importer, is taken off the list and never sold to again.

I have tasted at Domaine des Comtes Lafon only a few times over the years, but each time has been memorable. I well remember one time not that long ago when I was there with my longtime colleague, Burgundy expert Peter Vezan. Just before we were going to the cellar to start the tasting, a large, brand-new Mercedes pulled up sporting Parisian 75 on its license plate. Two well-dressed, important-looking men in their fifties stepped out and came over to us. They explained to Dominique that they were surgeons from Paris and they would like to buy some of his wine, any of his wine. Dominique, who is about five feet eight inches tall, rail thin but sturdy with an aquiline nose, was wearing jeans and a sweater with a jacket at the ready for when we were to descend down to his very cold cellar. He listened patiently to the men, who were nearly abject in their pleas, and slowly shook his head no. All of his wine was already allocated; there was none for sale to them. Tails between their legs, they slowly walked back to their car and took off. I said to myself at the time, this man is the king of his castle, ruthlessly ruling his domaine.

There is good reason why his wines are so sought after. Lafon's white wines are consistently among the best in all of Burgundy. The reds, mostly from Volnay, are superb as well. Lafon's vineyard placement in both Meursault and Volnay is among the best in each village. He now cultivates by using biodynamic principles and uses neither herbicides nor chemical sprays, thereby protecting and preserving the soil.

It is important to note, Lafon has one of the deepest and coldest cellars in Burgundy. This may partially explain why his white wines especially have such amazing depth and complexity, with the extraordinary ability to age and improve over a long period of time. I can attest to that longevity. Some years back my daughter, Erica, who was living in Paris at the time, was looking for an interesting birthday present for me but was stymied. She went to her friend and neighbor Peter Vezan for advice and assistance. Peter reluctantly, with some prompting from Erica, went to his personal cellar and sold her a bottle of 1989 Meursault Perrieres from Comtes Lafon. She gave it to me on my birthday, and I had it shortly thereafter. The wine was a deep but not dark golden honey in color. It had not a trace of oxidation. It was unusually concentrated but not viscous, crisp and amazingly fresh in its purity, superbly balanced, with deeply complex flavors of peach, honey, and even raspberries, with an intriguing nuttiness. The finish was silk, and the aftertaste went on for several minutes. Trust me, this description in no way does justice to that wine. I would never have guessed that it was over fifteen years old. This was the most red/white Burgundy I have ever had. Tried blind, one may very well have thought it to be a red wine. I tried to get Vezan to sell me another bottle, but no chance.

There is a way to occasionally get some Comtes Lafon wine. Dominique has owned vineyards in Burgundy's Mâcon region since 1999. Those holdings, located in the villages of Bussières, Chardonnay, Milly-Lamartine, and Uchizy, produce six outstanding, very fairly priced for the quality, 100 percent chardonnay. These, too, have had a loyal following and also sell out very quickly each year.

Tasting in Meursault at Domaine Albert Grivault

I love tasting at Domaine Albert Grivault. The white wines, from Bourgogne Blanc to Meursault Clos des Perrières, are always full of character, exhilarating, crisp, and among the best in the village. I particularly enjoy tasting with Monsieur Bardet. Michel Bardet, whom I only call Monsieur Bardet, is the grandson of Albert Grivault. He has been running the domaine for the past twenty years that I have been going there, although rumor has it that his daughter, Claire, and son, Henri-Marc, may soon be passed the baton.

M. Bardet is a very distinctive-looking individual of a certain age, I would guess around seventy-five years. He is a rather large fellow, well over six feet tall, large bodied but not corpulent, with a prominent proboscis and an enviable mane of pure white hair that he combs straight back. You would think that being in retail I would be good at recognizing people's faces and names, but that is not one of my strengths. That said, a few years back when I was taking the train to Chablis for tastings with Jean-Marc Brocard and at Domaine Long Depaquit, I was startled to see M. Bardet passing by on the corridor where I was seated. "Ah, M. Bardet," I exclaimed, "Comment allez-vous?" How are you, M. Bardet? "He responded, "M. Berman. C'est bien de vous voir." It's nice to see you. It was like the *Queen Elizabeth* passing me by. You couldn't miss him.

We always leave lots of extra time when visiting Domaine Albert Grivault. M. Bardet usually has many bottles already opened, some recently, some from a week ago. If we find that one opened previously is tired, he gets a fresh bottle and opens that too. There is no polite way to escape. As the domaine has only Bourgogne Blanc, Meursault Villages, Meursault 1er Cru Perrières, and Meursault 1er Cru Clos Perrières, along with their sole red, Pommard Clos Blanc, one would think we could get out of there quickly. Not even close. M. Bardet likes to compare various wines and various vintages, cross-checking them, if you will, expounding on the wines and their virtues. He speaks clear, not rapid, carefully enunciated French that is so well articulated I believe that even non-francophones would understand him perfectly well. He could have been a professor.

The Grivault wines are always marvelous and present an interesting contrast to those from Lafon. Whereas the Comte Lafon wines are steely and closed in their youth, tightly clenched and needing time, the Grivault wines are warmer and more open. They still have the requisite underlying strength that one would expect from great Meursault from a first-class domaine, but you can get into them earlier and enjoy them sooner. It may have been said, but if so I can't remember by whom, that some dogs (seem to) resemble their owners. So it can be, to some extent, with wine. The tight, closed-in wines from Lafon reflect Dominique's reticent, austere personality, whereas the openness and warmth, with a solid backbone, resemble more closely the voluble, ebullient personality of M. Bardet. It's a funny world.

While M. Bardet is too old to work the fields, he does have regular vineyard workers, vignerons, who get paid by the job and are not on the clock full time. This is not a large domaine, only about six hectares, around fourteen or so acres, so the vineyard work is not that physically demanding. Grivot's Meursault Clos Perrières is a *monopole* of the domaine, meaning it is exclusive to them, a monopoly if you will. It is a fabulous wine from a parcel located smack dab in the middle of the Meursault 1er Cru Perrières vineyard. It is considered by many to be the best Meursault, every vintage. In fact, M. Bardet has applied for a status change to Grand Cru for the Clos Perrières and an upgrade to Meursault for his Bourgogne Blanc. Good luck with that in stodgy Burgundy. Clos Perrières, however, is a fabulous wine, one that I have been offering since the 2004 vintage. I do believe it may be of Grand Cru caliber with its subtle wood, crisp acidity, and long, mineral-tinged flavors, but the odds of it receiving Grand Cru status are very long indeed. Of course, he won't know if he doesn't try. Anyway, I love all the Albert Grivault whites, and the quality level from the entry-level Bourgogne Blanc on up the line is very high.

Tasting with Olivier Leflaive

As noted, Bonnie didn't come on too many wine-buying trips with me because, even taking it easy, it can be grueling. I usually go from early morning until late at night. For this trip I planned a tasting with Olivier Leflaive. Olivier's home and domaine are a one-minute walk from the auberge where I like to stay when in Burgundy, La Chouette in Puligny, so tasting there was easy.

Domaine Leflaive must be included among the handful of the greatest white Burgundy producers, along with Domaine Comtes Lafon, Coche-Dury, Guy Roulot, and the irascible Jean Marie Guffens. Although Olivier was a member of the famous Puligny family, Leflaive, he separated from them and started his own negotiant firm. Olivier was in his midforties at the time of this visit, not too tall, five foot nine or so, and not fat but not lean. I found him to be amusing and very bright. He used to speak English with me, and I would answer back in French. Bonnie and I arrived at his cellar late morning, and we both had miserable colds. It is no fun tasting with a cold, but we went through the whole gamut of Leflaive wines anyhow, both domaine wines and Olivier's *negotiant* selections. I particularly liked his Bourgogne Blanc Les Setilles for its price/quality ratio. I told Olivier that if he were to import some, I'd be a buyer. He did, and I was his first customer for the wine in the US. It has been very successful for them over the years.

A huge benefit of tasting with Olivier this time was that we also got to taste samples from the whole range of Domaine Leflaive wines, which are kept completely separate from Olivier's *négociant* wines. Domaine Leflaive's 1er Crus, including Puligny-Montrachet les Folatieres, Puligny-Montrachet les Pucelles, Grands Crus, Bienvenues Batard Montrachet, Batard Montrachet, and Chevalier Montrachet, were simply breathtakingly fabulous wines. It was easy to discern their extraordinary qualities even with a cold.

We were supposed to go out to lunch with Olivier, but something came up that he had to deal with. He told us, "There's a little restaurant a few miles (six km) from Puligny heading toward Beaune. Please go there, and the lunch is on me." I thanked him, and he added, "Take any of the open bottles that we have been tasting to have with your lunch, your choice." Grinning at him, I said, "Olivier, you know what I am going to choose, the 1983 Chevalier Montrachet." "I figured as much," he said with a laugh.

The restaurant, which was located on the left side of the road on the main route going from Puligny to Beaune, is still there: L'Auberge du Vieux Vigneron. It was very Burgundian, rustic and charming, with lots of flowers, as this was in May. The food was good, a warm and rustic *coq au vin* and *salade*, but the wine, WOW! As I said, we had colds, but it didn't matter. The viscous honeyed flavor of the fabulous Leflaive Chevalier Montrachet (100 percent chardonnay) just trickled down our throats, coating our palates with gobs of extract and glycerin. The year 1983 was a hot vintage year, and the Leflaives made white wines that were so concentrated that, with eyes closed, one might very well think the wine was red, not white. We slowly and quite happily finished the bottle with our lunch and went off to our next appointment, perhaps not cured but feeling less pain.

Beaune: Hotel Le Cep

The next day was gray and overcast with sporadic rain showers. We made all of our appointments but although our colds were better, we were still suffering with them. We were staying at a wonderful old hotel in the center of Beaune called Le Cep. With some additions and modernizations over the years it still is an ideal, if not *the* ideal, place to stay when visiting Beaune and the region. As we were both tired and not that hungry, we left the car at the hotel and walked up the street to look for a place where we could have a quiet, not grand, lunch. We saw a likely restaurant not too far from the hotel, which, upon entering, seemed to be a bit fancier than we wanted or had expected from the exterior. We were greeted by a lovely lady, maybe midforties and stunning. She politely asked if we wanted to be seated for lunch. We said yes but explained that we only wanted a bowl of soup, if that was OK. She said that, no, that wasn't possible, so sorry, and recommended another restaurant farther down the square that could accommodate us.

The weather was beginning to look nasty, spitting a bit of rain and getting darker. It must have been obvious that we had colds, because before we left she stopped us. "Attendez," she said. Please wait a minute. "Where is your umbrella? The weather is deteriorating." We explained that we left it at the hotel. "You are staying at Le Cep?" she inquired. "Yes," we answered. She told us to wait a minute and went and got her own, personal, not inexpensive umbrella. "Here, take this," she said. "If I am not at the restaurant when you come back, just leave it at the charcuterie next door."

The French, often deservedly, take flack from us. But I have found that if you treat people, any people, with respect with a good attitude, they will respond in kind. For the most part French people have always treated me well. Sure, I have had some incidents, but those could have happened in New York, Boston, or even a town like Lexington. People are much the same the world 'round. Big-city inhabitants are different and act differently from those who live in the country.

A Funny/Scary Adventure in Pernand Vergelesses

Thirty years ago, before I started Arborway Imports, I used to travel to France with colleagues in the business. It was an opportunity for the importers I traveled with to introduce me to their suppliers and taste me on their wines, with the hope of making some sales. In Burgundy we often tasted cask samples of the latest vintage. It was good for them, as the wines and prices spoke for themselves and needed no sales pitch. And it was a great opportunity for me to learn trends, what was hot, what was not, and taste and select wines before they ever hit the market, and at special volume pricing.

This particular trip was one of my first such excursions. I was working with an importer about my own age that we will call "Barry." Barry and I were traveling with Peter Griffiths, an English courtier who was based in France and specialized in Burgundies. Peter was in his early to midthirties, five feet ten or so, with a very fair complexion, blonde, and beefy. He was kind of a know-it-all wise guy. Cheeky, the English would say. I wasn't overly fond of him, but he had great contacts. After working hard Monday through Friday in Burgundy, we intended to leave for Bordeaux early Saturday morning, as it was an eight-and-a-half-hour drive. This was not to be. Griffiths got an unbreakable appointment at Domaine Bonneau du Matray, one of Burgundy's most prestigious properties, whose Corton Charlemagne is among the very best. Barry and I were more than a little upset. This messed up all of our plans, and leaving midafternoon would make the drive to Bordeaux less than pleasant.

Since there was nothing that could be done about it except excoriate Peter, which we did, we got some ham and cheese sandwiches, a couple of sixes of John Courage beer, and went up to the hills of Corton for a picnic. The early June weather was spectacular, and we enjoyed the sandwiches and beer until it was time to deposit Griffiths at the domaine. In case you didn't know, John Courage is *not* Budweiser. This beer packs a punch, and so we were all—well, maybe not Griffiths—feeling quite relaxed. Barry and I dropped him off and drove to a shaded side street off the quiet main road in Pernand Vergelesses to wait.

Here's where the fun begins. There's no way you could do this today, but thirty years ago Barry used to bring in a pack of "fatties" hidden under his sock. Today a beagle would have chewed his leg off before he went to jail. Once we were comfortably situated under a tree on a shaded street, he pulled out a joint that would have made Cheech and Chong proud. After he lit up and had a couple of hits he turned, gave me a piercing look, and said, "Want some?" I had been such a good trooper so far on this trip, very conservative and focused. I looked at him and the fatty and said, "Sure." Took a hit, passed it back, had a couple more, and was feeling mellow. Just then, a young girl probably nine or ten years old walked by. This is a tiny village. Everybody knows everybody. It must have been more than disconcerting for her to see two sinister-looking strangers sitting in a car on her street, on such a beautiful day. We looked at her, she looked at us, and I realized—I don't think it was marijuana-induced paranoia—she was absolutely terrified. I turned to Barry and said, "We've got to get out of here. They'll be coming after us with pitchforks."

"Where will we go?" he asked. "I'm not sure I can find my way back." I said, "We're at the top of the hill. Just go, right, right, right, and to get back we'll just reverse ourselves, continuing left. So we did just that and ended up down on the flat, where we could look at the Route Nationale. Of course, we could have been seen from there as well, but we weren't bothered. The joint was wearing down fast. I may have had another hit but not more. We were both a bit shaken up by our encounter with the girl. When I knew it was getting close to time to pick up Griffiths, I turned to Barry and suggested that we leave. Then I took a good look at him and said, "Barry, look at your eyes. They are slits." He took the rearview mirror, turned it so that I could see myself, and said, "Look at your own." Uh oh. They looked like two cherries in a bowl of buttermilk. Not good.

We wended our way left and found ourselves outside Bonneau du Matray. Barry said, "Go knock on the door, ask for Griffiths, and tell him to get his butt out here so we can leave."

I now know why they call it "stoned." I felt five hundred pounds heavy. I said, "No way. He's your courtier. I'm just along for the ride. Besides, I can't move." Barry gave me a filthy look, got out of the car, and hit the knocker, glaring at me all the while. Me, I was highly amused. After a minute or so the owner of the domaine, Count de la Moriniere, opened the door. The tasting was not finished, so he invited us both in. The devilish look on Barry's face as he beckoned me to descend and enter was priceless. Sweet revenge.

Griffiths, who was no dope and wise to Barry's propensities, must have informed the count in advance that we had been drinking beer earlier and that the "Americans" may be a bit "tipsy." The count, then in his midsixties, was obviously a military man. He comported himself as such with perfect, straight-back posture. He was maybe five eleven, very thin but not slight. He welcomed us in fractured, almost incomprehensible English, which he liked to employ, although he understood not one word of our responses. It was apparent that he was aristocratic from his bearing and by how pleased he was with himself. Why not? He was a count, his property was magnificent, and so was his wine.

Back then, neither Barry nor I was impressed with his aristocracy. Nearly everything he did cracked us up. It was on us, not him, but I felt like I was back in high school, sitting far back in class stifling laughter, where a substitute teacher was being harassed by the kids up front. Every time the count tried to speak English we found it hilarious. I had to bite my tongue to keep from laughing out loud. That doesn't mean that the state we were in wasn't apparent.

The count took the pipette to make a blend of Corton Charlemagne, a bit from an old wooden barrel, some from one that was new. I don't know why, but I found his exaggerated gestures in doing this perfectly normal cellar activity unbelievably funny. We were just barely holding it together when, mercifully, the tasting was finished.

As we were leaving the cave, saying our goodbyes, we walked out into gorgeous sunlight. Barry got behind the wheel, I was shotgun, and Griffiths went in the back. The perplexed count seemed stymied. He looked from Barry to Peter and back again. The driver's-side window was down and the count, military man that he was, made a tactical error. He put his hand on Barry's arm and said, "Don't you think that Peter should drive?" Barry snarled at him, "What's the matter? Are you afraid you'll lose your courtier?" And off he drove, heading for Bordeaux. Not our finest moment.

Once we hit the autoroute it was obvious that the count was 100 percent correct. Barry's driving was erratic and staccato. One minute he'd be going an easy 140 KM, two minutes later, 160 KM, then 130. Finally, I turned to him and said, "Look, I'm straight as an arrow. Why don't you pull over, go in the back, and get some sleep. I'll drive for a while." And that's what we did.

Côte Chalonnaise

Givry

The Côte Chalonnaise is a beautiful, wooded, area off the beaten path in Burgundy that is neat to visit and explore. There are no worries about having to fight other tourists for space, and there are some excellent wineries that are fun and informative to visit. Located south of the Côte d'Or and north of Beaujolais and Mâcon, but easily accessible to both, it is a charming, sparsely populated, wooded, rather hilly region of Burgundy. It has more open space and is somewhat less manicured than the famous Côte d'Or regions to the north.

Because the Côte Chalonnaise vineyards are further south, their pinot noir and chardonnay grapes can ripen faster than their northern counterparts. Therefore the vintage usually takes place earlier, often avoiding the potentially damaging storms that can occur later in the season. Burgundies, white and red, from the Côte Chalonnaise Villages fly under the radar and are excellent values. Their villages may be less well known than Pommard, Gevrey Chambertin, Chassagne Montrachet, Meursault, etc., but many of the Côte Chalonnaise growers offer wines that can successfully compete with those better-known villages with wines that can be their equal at far lower prices.

There are five wine-producing communes in the Côte Chalonnaise: Bouzeron, Rully, Mercurey, Givry, and Montagny. Montagny produces only white wine, and while many are very good, I wish they cost just a little less. I have never found one to import. Bouzeron is noted for the white-grape variety Aligoté. I am not a fan; forgive me. But the other three offer some terrific, very fairly priced red and white Burgundies, a number of which are 1er Crus.

My favorite domaine in the region is Domaine Michel Sarrazin et Fils, located in Givry (pronounced "GEEvree"), not to be confused with the "Gevrey" (pronounced "gehVRAY") of Gevrey Chambertin. When visiting the domaine, I always spend some time with the very personable Guy (pronounced Ghee) Sarrazin. I rarely see his brother, Jean-Yves, as he is usually in the fields, but he is always pleasant as well.

The Sarrazin brothers were brought up in the wine business. It was understood that they would one day take over from their dad and, hopefully, expand the enterprise, which they have. Vineyard work is brutal, and it's a hard life. Most vignerons/farmers retire early if they can and let the younger generation take over. The Sarrazin vineyards are located in the tiny hamlet of Jambles (pronounced zhamBLAYe). It's not even big enough to be called a village, as only five hundred or so souls reside there. It is not exactly a tourist attraction either. As many times as we have been to the domaine, it always takes an effort to find our way there. What is most noteworthy about this place for wine lovers are the surrounding high-altitude vineyards good for growing high-quality grapes. There is an obvious quality difference between wines produced from the hillside AOC Givry vines (*appellation d'origine contrôlée*) when compared to those from less fortunately placed flatland vineyards.

There is a perhaps surprising range of wines to be tried at Sarrazin each visit, both red and white. Unless I carefully triage the offerings, I will be there for hours. While they have three or four very nice whites, I have never bought one. It's their red wines that shake my tree. Their Bourgogne Rouge, which comes from vineyards just outside of the Givry *appellation*, is always delicious. Current vintages are saturated ruby in color, with lovely aromas of raspberries and cassis fruit, delicious dark berry flavors tinged with cinnamon spice. Usually drinkable upon release, it is smooth on the palate and surprisingly inexpensive, especially when compared to the prices asked for Côte de Nuits Bourgognes Rouge.

Regardless of how many wines Guy has me taste, I have always found his single-vineyard Givry Champs Lalot to be the best wine in his cellar, equal to any of his 1er Crus or better. *Le Guide Hachette des Vins*, one of France's oldest and most respected wine guides, was aware of the qualities of Givry Champs Lalot well before me and has many times conferred on it their highest award, *coup de cœur 3 étoiles*. Shockingly, because this is such a rare occurrence, starting with the 2012 vintage, Givry-Champs Lalot was elevated to 1er Cru status, no small feat and very rare. However, only the upper part of the vineyard was designated as 1er Cru. The lower half could have still been called Champs Lalot and could be labeled as such, but without the 1er Cru designation. Interestingly, Guy Sarrazin, I believe correctly and honestly, decided to differentiate between the two halves by calling one Givry 1er Cru Champs Lalot and the other half Givry Les Dracy. Therefore there should be no confusion between the two. But both are from the exact same vineyard.

Givry Champs Lalot is the bigger and deeper of the two, but Givry Les Dracy will drink better earlier and perhaps not live quite as long. I imported both these wines, as they are irresistibly delicious. There was no way to pass up the small amount of each allocated to me. I would have always doubled my order if I could. They both offer Sarrazin's signature style. Bigger and fuller-bodied than Sarrazin's excellent Bourgogne Rouge, these are fresh, concentrated, and long on the palate. It is not unusual to see Sarrazin's wines on the lists of various French temples of gastronomy, like Taillevent, as well as some of New York's top restaurants. Any wine with Sarrazin on the label is worth ordering.

Lunch with Guy Sarrazin

I had just completed a very successful visit with Guy Sarrazin while working with my colleague and friend Charles Blagden, an expatriate Englishman who has lived in France for over thirty years. It was a beautiful June day. Guy insisted that we all go out to lunch with him. He knew of a restaurant close by, not out of our way, that had good food with relatively quick service, and we could eat outdoors. "Sure," we said, "let's go." Traveling with me then was my retail store manager, Mal, on his first trip to France. It was very quickly found out that Mal was squeamish about much of the food served, and with reason: he had a weak stomach. I have to admit, I am apprehensive about some of it too, but manage.

We were seated outside at a rectangular table, with Charles on one side facing Guy and Mal and me on the other. Frankly, *tête de veau* and *pied de porc* do not tempt me at all, but Guy and Charles love them. Fortunately, there was *boeuf* Bourguignon on the menu, so I said to Mal, "I will order for you a green salad and *boeuf* Bourguignon so you will be fine. Don't even look to see what the others are eating. OK?" Our food was fine rustic cuisine with delicious, crusty bread. But I actually had to set up a barrier so that Mal couldn't see what the others had been served and were eagerly digging into, as Mal took one look and turned white. Neither Guy nor Charles was aware of Mal's discomfort, and neither missed a beat either talking or eating. Not that they would have cared had they known. It may seem amusing now, but it was less so at the time, especially for Mal.

Mercurey

Like Givry, Mercurey is another underrated Côte Chalonnaise village whose wines often fly under the radar but shouldn't. I didn't have a Mercurey in my portfolio and wanted to import one, so I asked Guy Sarrazin if he had someone to recommend. He suggested I go see Domaine Jean Maréchale, located maybe twenty minutes away from his winery. Jean Maréchale and his huge, very friendly, ex-basketball-playing son-in-law, the aptly named Jean Bonvigne, make an extensive range of wines from Mercurey, including several 1er Crus. However, their Mercurey 1er Cru Clos l'Eveque, while not the most expensive wine they offer, is always their best, every vintage. They changed their vinification method a few years ago to provide a plumper, richer style of wine with no loss of finesse, and the wines, while always good, are better than ever. Current vintages are not as hard as they were in the past but will still age beautifully. Produced from vines aged fifty-five to sixty years, this wine invariably has a dark purple color and excellent concentration, style, and depth. It is supple, with youthful tannins, long, intense flavors of black raspberry/cassis, black cherry, and plums. It is a delicious wine that can be drunk young but will live and improve for several more years after the vintage. It is always very fairly priced for a 1er Cru. Would that all recommendations work out so well.

Cru Beaujolais

What Is Cru Beaujolais?

Beaujolais is located south of Mâcon and north of Lyon. The land is made up of rolling hills dotted with small houses planted into the hillsides, surrounded by vines. It is one of the most beautiful areas in all of France. All red Beaujolaises, unlike other red Burgundies, which are 100 percent pinot noir, are made 100 percent from Gamay grapes.

To be clear, qualitatively Beaujolais Villages and Cru Beaujolais have nothing in common with Beaujolais Nouveau. The latter is more akin to grape juice than wine, while the former are serious wines, if somewhat fun loving. Beaujolais classifies its vineyard sites. The wines of ordinary vineyards are simply labeled "Beaujolais." Vineyards in higher-ranked villages can label their wines as "Beaujolais-Villages." Those wines tend to offer more substance than the rarely seen basic Beaujolais. They have more complex flavors and more structure. Vineyards in the ten villages designated as Beaujolais Crus can label their wines with the "Cru" name only, so, for example, Brouilly or Julienas rather than just Beaujolais Village.

Cru Beaujolais represent the best of Beaujolais, offering serious, delicious, and, often, age-worthy wines. They don't get nearly the attention they deserve from wine lovers despite their drinkability and excellent price-to-quality ratio. Beaujolais appellations such as Morgon, Chiroubles, Moulin-a-Vent, and Côtes de Brouilly may not be household Burgundy names, like Gevrey-Chambertin or Pommard. However, due to the success of recent vintages, and word of mouth from people who have visited this beautiful, hilly region, these wines are becoming better known, yet still not well-known enough. This is a pity, because it seems that every year we find new, high-quality, dynamic producers and import their wines, often only to just languish. Like the Mâconnais, far too many hardworking growers are living paycheck to paycheck, and most are staring bankruptcy in the face. Not a fun way to live and wholly undeserving.

Most Beaujolais is at its best when it is no more than two or three years old; this is when it is at its fruitiest and freshest. But the crus can live and improve for several years and do what the French call *pinote*, which is to transform to become more pinot noir (Burgundian) like.

If you think Beaujolais is characterized by Beaujolais nouveau, then please try some of their Crus; they will be a revelation.

The
Mâconnais

Tasting at Domaine Auvigue

While the Côte d'Or whites to the north—Meursault, Puligny-Montrachet, Chassagne Montrachet, etc.—get well-deserved rave reviews for their quality, there are many Mâconnais estates, including Domaine Auvigue, that make wines that compete qualitatively at significantly lower prices. The Auvigue family holdings date back to 1629, when they had vineyards in both Beaujolais and the Mâconnais. They have been working their vineyards for generations, today using traditional Burgundian methods but with updated ideas and new equipment. The grapes for the most part come from the family's own extensive holdings. However, they do buy carefully selected grapes from a few contracted growers who own vineyards in the best areas of the Pouilly-Fuissé, Saint Véran, and Mâcon appellations. Two of my favorite Auvigue wines are their Mâcon Solutré, which has always been cultivated by organic farming methods, and their Pouilly-Fuissé Cuvée Naturelle vineyard, which since 2009 has been as well.

I have been importing wines from Jean-Pierre Auvigue for over twenty-five years, and it is always one of my favorite stops when in Burgundy. It's often my last stop, because the TGV (*Train Gran Vitesse*), France's bullet train, has a station at Mâcon Charnay, only minutes from the Auvigue estate. I very often take that train back to Paris after a week in Burgundy.

Jean-Pierre Auvigue is of medium height, slight but wiry with a thin face with sharp, not unpleasant, features. I have great admiration and affection for Jean-Pierre. He is intelligent, hardworking, personable, and nice. He has been working at the domaine since he could walk. He once told me, as he was driving me around his family's vast Mâcon holdings, that he was once married. It lasted a year. He now says he is married to his domaine and the craft of making the greatest wine he is capable of. There is no thirty-five-hour work week for guys like Jean-Pierre. He works between sixty and eighty hours a week and has total disdain for the regulations and the bureaucratic morass he and growers like him are compelled to deal with.

All the growers with whom I work feel the same way, and many vocally express their contempt for the system. It's serious and not fun and games. Philippe Delarche, based in Pernand Vergelesses, was hounded for years by the authorities for a paper snafu that they refused to acknowledge and fix, meaning he had fines to pay. Philippe, sadly, died of brain cancer in 2008. He may have succumbed to the disease then anyway, but I am sure the pressure he felt exacerbated his condition and quickened his demise. Their domaine remains in the good hands of his son, Etienne, but the loss of Philippe is still painful and sad.

Jean-Pierre is quick, bright, and intuitive. He often offers some interesting points of view on the Burgundy wine scene in general and, of course, Mâcon especially. Tasting with him is always a bit drawn out, as he makes four or five different Mâcons, a few different Saint Vérans, and a half-dozen or so Pouilly-Fuissés. Why so many? First of all, he has a market for each wine, and they all have varying degrees of diversity. Some have no wood, like his terrific Mâcon Villages and even better Mâcon Davayé. He has other wines that are more heavily wooded, like some of his single-vineyard Pouilly-Fuissés. There is something there for everyone. Even though we always have at least twenty wines to taste, some from different vintages, as well as wines in cask, Jean Pierre goes through them with relative alacrity. This is not at all the norm at most Burgundy estates. Often we will go with him for lunch and take some of the open bottles with us to have at one of the modest, rustic, but good restaurants in the area. It is always great to share them with him at the table and see how they go with food. All of his wines are worthy and offer quality at a price.

That said, I have consistently only bought four wines from Auvigue over the years: his much-beloved crystalline, nonwooded Mâcon Davayé from day one. More recently I have added his lovely Viré-Clessé, Mâcon-Solutré, and his Pouilly-Fuissé Cuvée Naturelle. Each of these wines has its own charm and individual character.

The Mâconnais would be a great place to vacation or just visit when in Burgundy. It is less than two hours from Paris by the fast train (TGV). Located south of Beaune, Puligny, and Meursault, it is north of and not far from Beaujolais and its gorgeous rolling hills. It is never overrun with tourists, so there are charming inns and B and Bs that are affordable and welcoming. Heading north to the Côte de Beaune or Côte D'Or is easy by the regional, scenic routes or quickly via autoroute. There are a number of local restaurants that would be fun to dine at, especially on Sunday afternoons, where you could mingle with families of the hardworking citizenry. Also, one could head for Chagny, a half-hour or so away, and dine at the justly acclaimed three-star restaurant Lameloise. I wouldn't necessarily go to the Mâconnais in the dead of winter, but late spring, when the flowers start to bloom, or early fall, when the leaves turn would be delightful.

Dining at Lameloise-Chagny (Macon) France

My first experience at Lameloise was certainly memorable. In the early 1980s, when I first started traveling to France on wine-buying trips, my dining experiences in top restaurants were nil. At that time, the now defunct Hill Top in Saugus or Anthony's equally defunct Pier Four were more likely places we would opt to go for a special night out.

On one of my earliest buying trips to Burgundy, in the mid-1980s, I was excited to go to the famed three-star restaurant Lameloise with colleagues. The restaurant, located in Chagny, south of Puligny and just north of Macon, was and is an unpretentious Michelin three-star restaurant. They feature brilliantly prepared and served traditional French cuisine. I was, frankly, more than a bit in awe, as I was unaccustomed to dining in such establishments. On my own I wouldn't have dared to go. My traveling companions, however, had dined there several times and were psyched.

Although Lameloise may, perhaps, have then lacked the elegance of Taillevent or Jamin, it had its own rustic charm. The service was spot on, and the accoutrements were impeccable. I perused the menu and ordered *coquilles* Saint Jacques as a starter. There were six of us at the table, and all were enjoying the food and wine. I took a bite of my *coquilles*. Mmm, delicious, I loved it! I took another bite and, uh oh, I spat out a (not small) piece of glass. Evidently, a glass had broken in the kitchen and a piece had flown up to my plate undetected. Should they have caught it? Absolutely. It could have been the end of me.

While I was looking astounded at the piece of glass in my hand, the rest of the table glared at me as if it were my fault. I guess they thought I should have swallowed it! Not so the waiters. They were mortified, and I was embarrassed. They made a huge fuss and insisted on offering a starter of turbot instead of the coquilles. I tried to tell them that I *really* wanted the coquilles, as what I tasted of it initially was great, but no. They were adamant that turbot was what I was getting, and that was that.

Their sommelier, Georges, who had been there for years, had a little game for us to play. This was my first time, but my friends were nonplussed, as they had been there and done this more than once before. Georges would pick a wine, invariably Burgundy, for us to try blind, and if we could guess what village it was from and the vintage, no charge. Georges won again that night. The wine was an excellent, elegant Nuits Saint Georges 1er Cru that tasted far more Vosne than Nuits. We never had a chance.

Some years later, I took Bonnie on one of my Burgundy buying trips and reserved a table at Lameloise. I can't remember what wine I ordered that night but do remember what we had for dinner. Usually it's the other way around. Anyway, I uncharacteristically ordered *pigeonneau*, which was really guinea hen or squab, not pigeon. This was offered in a black-truffle sauce, so I was seduced. Bonnie ordered a chicken dish.

After we had finished our main course and were about to order a dessert, the waiter came by to ask if we were pleased with our meal. We almost never complain or send food back to the kitchen. Maybe if I get old enough I will learn. The waiter turned to me and said, "Le diner vous a plu?" Did the dinner please you? I said, "Oui," as my dinner was terrific. Then he asked if Bonnie was equally pleased. "Madame egalement?" In fact she was not. She found her meal to be bland and a bit boring. I said to the waiter, "En effet, non. Elle étais déçue." No, she was disappointed. I further explained that we had expected more from such a storied restaurant. Horrified, he asked, "Would she like us to make something else?" No, thank you anyway, and we ordered dessert, which was delicious.

Then we saw our waiter heading for our table with something else. "Excuse me," I said. "We didn't order that." "I know," said the waiter, "but the chef felt badly that you weren't happy with your meal, so he wanted to send you this to make up for it." It was a tangerine crème brulée that was one of the best, certainly most memorable, desserts that either of us had ever had. That's how a classy establishment deals with customers who may be dissatisfied, and that's how they keep them coming back, to this day.

Dining at Georges Blanc in Vonnas

Even before I went to Lameloise, my first truly memorable dining experience was at Georges Blanc, located in Vonnas, France, a *village fleurie*, or flowered village, in the Mâconnais. The main industry of this town located just north of Beaujolais was, you guessed it, the three-star restaurant Georges Blanc. It has now expanded far beyond just offering a wonderful dining experience. It now includes an elegant fine hotel with top-class spa treatments available. Back in the early '80s it was a more modest Michelin-starred restaurant where rooms were available. But the reason to go there was the food.

I was then traveling to Burgundy for the first time with the owner and GM of a small, quality-oriented import company We had been working for a week tasting, evaluating, and selecting wines to potentially buy. I know that many people would say, "Working?" Well, yes.

We get up early and are on the road at eight thirty or so each morning and work until eight thirty at night, and then go to dinner and discuss who we saw and what we, hopefully, liked over a glass or two of wine. We often have many miles to go to get to our next appointment, and we are invariably late, as each winemaker insists that we try just one more wine. "Il faut que vous goutiez ça!" It's pretty hard to extricate yourself without being rude. The next grower knows the drill, so it's basically all good, but very time consuming and tiring. Today, cell phones help, big time.

My colleagues were well acquainted with Georges Blanc's restaurant and felt that after the long work week, we deserved a treat. We stayed at a nondescript, inexpensive hotel not far away from Georges Blanc, apparently to save money for the wine list.

I had never been to a French temple of gastronomy or even dreamed one might exist. The restaurant was beautifully appointed, with lovely flower arrangements everywhere. The service was precise, unpretentious, and knowledgeable. I have no recollection as to what I was served on their *menu dégustation* but do remember that the amuse-bouches were amazing. They were especially exciting to me, as they were unexpected and I had never been served anything like them before.

We scoured the encyclopedic wine list and then called over the extremely erudite young English sommelier. They had a relatively reasonable price on a 1955 Leroy Gevrey Chambertin 1er Cru les Cazetiers. Of course, it wasn't inexpensive, but three of us were splitting the bill. My colleagues were decided and went for it. Frankly, back then, I doubt if I knew about Leroy wines, and I would never have dared to order one if I did. I subsequently found out that Madame Lalou Bize-Leroy was at that time partners at Domaine de la Romanée Conti (DRC), with Aubert de Villaine comanaging the estate. She also sold some then legendary wines under the Leroy label. They still are. Grapes from her vineyards have very low yields and are produced biodynamically. The wines were and are astronomically expensive. I am told that they are worth it but, unfortunately, I have never had another of her wines.

She had a series of fallings out with Aubert in the early '90s and was ousted from the DRC in 1992.

To say that the '55 Leroy Cazetiers was a revelation wouldn't do it justice. This was a nearly thirty-year-old wine. It had such deep color, depth, and power that one would have thought it was eight or ten years old. We actually called the sommelier over and questioned its provenance. "Is this really a '55?" we asked. He laughed and said, "You should try the '53 next time." We undoubtedly had other wine that night, but I don't recall which. What I do remember quite fondly are the *mignardises*, which were so delicious that I would have eaten everything on the dessert tray if my friends hadn't finally dragged me away, protesting all the while.

I went back to Georges Blanc some years later with my wife, Bonnie. I had begun my import company, Arborway Imports, and was representing and distributing the Cremant de Bourgogne Georges Blanc, along with a few other of his wines. The Cremant was a very nice, fairly priced Champagne lookalike with which we had some success. So much so that I was invited to stay at their hotel and have dinner at Georges Blanc when next in France. Bonnie and I were excited and planned to go after a brief Paris vacation, as this would be a unique and special experience. And so it turned out to be.

We got there midmorning and were warmly welcomed. We were asked if we would like to have lunch at Georges Blanc's sister restaurant about twelve kilometers away in the city of Mâcon. We said, "That would be lovely. Thank you." It was an endearing and less formal restaurant than its more illustrious sister, with very friendly staff. Before ordering, Bonnie explained to the waiter that she had numerous food allergies, most particularly shellfish and, especially, lobster. We ordered and, when the food arrived, Bonnie took one bite and grimaced. I knew she was in trouble. Lobster had been surreptitiously added to the sauce! How could they do that? Who knows, but they did. My poor wife was very ill and couldn't eat even bread for dinner.

To say I was bummed out would be putting it mildly. Here I was with my wife at one of France's greatest restaurants, and I would have to dine by myself. And that I did. I may not have been happy about it, but that didn't affect my appetite. Their *menu dégustation* was beyond amazing; every dish was delicious. What did I drink? Showing them no mercy, I ordered a bottle of Henri Jayer 1986 Vosne Romanée 1er Cru Cros Parantoux. I drank nearly the whole bottle, the only wine from Henri Jayer I have ever had, and it was great! It had layer upon layer of gorgeous pinot complexity, with a heady aroma and a silky finish. Just the epitome of elegance and finesse, coupled with subtle power. 1986 was *not* a "great" Burgundy vintage, but it didn't matter. This was Jayer, and it was a great bottle. Although she was a trooper and kept me company at the table, I was still very upset that Bonnie couldn't enjoy the dining experience with me.

Chablis

I probably drink more than twice as much Chablis as I do any other white Burgundy. I love the steely, bone-dry minerality overlaid with flavors of stone and seashells that are found in the best of them. Chardonnay grown elsewhere cannot ever taste like real Chablis produced in the *appellation d'origine contrôlée* (AOC) Chablis region. It is unfortunate that so many usurpers of the Chablis name have muddied the waters, causing confusion in consumers who, not knowing any better, shun these great wines. Chablis's image is better today, as I don't believe that pink Chablis is still made. I certainly hope not. That was such a disservice to the hardworking Chablis growers who produce their unique brand of chardonnay, and residual damage remains.

Chablis, the northernmost wine district in Burgundy, is located halfway between the Côte d'Or and Paris, with vineyards planted nearly exclusively with chardonnay. The Chablis area was very heavily bombed during WWII, which did a number on the vineyards and the Chablis wine industry. Being resilient, however, they survived, although life is never easy for these growers. Chablis is so much farther north from the Côte d'Or that they have a different, far colder microclimate than does their more southern Burgundy cousins, with different, often daunting exigencies. Frost is a constant concern, as there have been vintages where entire crops were lost to it. Just recently, in 2016 there was much damage with huge losses; up to 50 percent of the crop was lost to catastrophic hail and frost.

Also, what may be a great vintage weather-wise in Chablis may not be the same in the Côte d'Or, and vice versa. The terroir, made up of Kimmeridgian clay and chalky soil, is totally different from what is found in the Côte d'Or. You don't even have to walk the vineyards to see that millions of years ago Chablis was at the bottom of an ocean. Just driving around, you can see an amazing amount of seashells and fossils covering the vineyards. Some shells disintegrated over time, nourishing the alluvial soil with an impossible-to-duplicate mineral richness. No other wines can taste just like Chablis, and it's easy to see why.

Chablis, like wines from other regions of Burgundy, has multiple tastes and styles, depending on the vineyard site and the grower, yet still unquestionably retains its distinctive Chablis character. I have been working with three Chablis domains: Jean Marc Brocard/Hervé Azo, Domaine Long-Depaquit, and Séguinot-Bordet. They all offer village Chablis, 1er Crus, and Grands Crus, and all three have different wine-making philosophies and styles. The wines from each of the three exemplify the domain style but also demonstrate the differences between each vineyard site within that context.

Jean Marc Brocard/Hervé Azo

Jean-Marc Brocard, the patriarch of the Brocard clan, has a quiet charisma that is clearly evident despite his booming welcome. Taller than medium height, with a florid face and a bit of girth, he is obviously self-assured and unquestionably in charge. I started importing Brocard's wine almost as soon as I had my import license in 1990. Five or six years back, Jean Marc came to see me in Lexington, to ask me a favor. The recession hit him hard. He had expanded too quickly based on how the economy was projected to be, not how it was after it fell out of bed. He was in a precarious position and decided, right or wrong, that the support of a national US distributor would give him added income and stability for his company. The problem for us was that the national distributor insisted on selling in all fifty states or none at all. So I was in the way in Massachusetts and could block the deal. Jean Marc explained the situation to me, and while I wasn't happy, after much discussion my son, Gregg, and I decided to step aside and not cause him further grief. We could have legally won the battle to retain the brand, but the war would have been lost if Brocard went out of business.

What Jean-Marc proposed to ease the pain was to give us the rights to import the Chablis from his Hervé Azo property as a substitute for the Brocard-labeled wines. Jean-Marc bought Azo in 2004, and the property included twelve hectares of prime Chablis vineyards. Nine of them were on excellent, sloped 1er Cru vineyard sites located around the village of Milly. They all had Kimmeridgian/limestone-rich soil heavily studded with prehistoric fossils. Brocard kept the domain intact and separate from his other properties, and kept the Hervé Azo name. Jean-Marc's son, Julien, began farming the properties in 2006 using organic/biodynamic methods.

While not happy in spite of the Azo Domaine's excellent array of vineyards, a few things finally convinced me to agree to the switch. First and foremost was that the Azo wines had the clear Brocard stamp that I so love. They are indisputably Chablis: crisp, with distinctive minerality and a taste of seashells, they are produced in a decidedly masculine style. Then Jean-Marc agreed to cut us a substantial discount for a few years to help us transition the Azo wines to customers who had been loyal to the Brocard brand. Lastly, I insisted that our order for Azo Bourgogne Blanc always be filled with Brocard's Chablis-like Bourgogne Blanc Kimmeridgian, which I love and had sold for years. It is Chablis in all but name. Likewise, the same may be said of his Sauvignon de Saint Bris. I insisted it be the Brocard Sauvignon de Saint Bris that I always bought. After he agreed to those terms, we began a new relationship, no less amicable. We never lost a sale or missed a beat.

Domaine Albert Bichot/Long-Depaquit

Maison Albert Bichot was founded in 1831. Like Louis Jadot, Joseph Drouhin, and Domaine Faiveley, it is a *négociant* firm. Albéric Bichot is the sixth-generation Bichot to run the domaine. He is a warm, capable man in his late forties, of medium height with a wiry frame. While much of their wine is produced from grapes bought from contracted growers, they also own many of their own vineyards, including some belonging to their subsidiary companies, which are part of Maison Albert Bichot. Aside from wines produced under the Bichot name they have Domaine du Pavillon in Pommard and Domaine du Clos Frantin in Vosne-Romanée. One of the absolute jewels of the domaine is their gorgeous Chablis property, Domaine Long-Depaquit. Founded in 1791, it is one of the larger Chablis estates, consisting of a whopping sixty-five hectares (160 acres) of vines. I have followed wines from Long-Depaquit for years, as they always made better than good wine. In the past several years, they have become infinitely better. Albéric has hired capable young vineyard managers and winemakers to ensure that the special terroir of his Crus Chablis are treated with the respect and care that they deserve, and to ensure that great wine will be made.

The Long-Depaquit style is no less "Chablis" than Brocard's Chablis from Hervé Azo; however, the wines are different in style. There is an easy-to-like creaminess to the wine, and it is decidedly less austere while still retaining the requisite crisp acidity and seashell notes. There is a full range of Chablis made at Long-Depaquit, from Petit Chablis to Grands Crus. Their magnificent *monopole* Chablis Grand Cru La Moutonne is always great wine, every vintage. The La Moutonne vineyard is located just between the Grand Cru vineyards of Les Preuses and Vaudésir. I have walked up the very steep hill to get to the top of this vineyard, where the view is spectacular and the air rarified. I must confide, for me it was easier to climb up than down. I never was a mountain goat, and with the shoes I was then wearing, I had to take care descending. Of course, the winemaker and regional representative Guillaume Suss, who I was with, bopped up and down with ease. If you do get to Chablis, the Château Long-Depaquit is a "must" to see and visit. It is unquestionably the most imposing edifice in Chablis.

Séguinot-Bordet

The third Chablis grower with whom I have worked is Jean François Bordet of Séguinot-Bordet. He has a much smaller domaine than either Bichot or Brocard, but he makes lovely Chablis that stylistically falls between the crisp austerity of Brocard and the softer Long-Depaquit style. The domaine, which dates back to 1590, consists of twenty-eight hectares of vineyards spread out in different sectors. Jean François is a slim, fit, nice-looking young man who looks to be slightly under thirty years of age. As soon as he finished school, he took over running the domaine from his grandfather, working hard in the vineyards to make sure that his grapes are as near perfect as possible each year. He is often a late harvester, which is a gamble that's worth it if the weather holds. Even with two Chablis domaines in my portfolio when introduced to him, I couldn't pass up his wines. I had to buy them even though I felt that I had enough Chablis at the time.

Chablis would be another neat, nontouristic region to visit for vacation. It's only 110 miles from Paris and around 80 miles from Beaune, but only thirty miles from Champagne. There are nineteen towns, and it's only 12 miles long, 9 miles wide. This is mostly farmland, so it's wide open and accessible. Getting there by car or by train is easy. There are a number of good, not expensive restaurants, and you won't pay Paris prices for either the food or the wine. I well remember dining with Jean Marc Brocard one evening at a nice, quaint local restaurant when I spotted a 2001 Chambolle Musigny from Roumier that was being offered at half the price I paid at a restaurant in Paris. Needless to say, we ordered the wine, and it was great.

The Why of Burgundy's Success

In the past, only five out of every ten Burgundy vintages were "good." Less than half of those were considered "great." Today nearly every vintage offers high-quality wines. This past decade, 2005, 2009, 2010, 2012, and 2015 were construed as being great vintages, and only 2004 was of just medium quality, and even those are showing well today. The rest—2006, 2007, 2008, 2011, 2013, and 2014—are all much better than good in their own way, with their own charm and style, and there were great wines produced in each of those vintages. The 2014 Côtes de Nuits wines are excellent, and the whites are great. Clive Coats has called 2014 "The best year ending in '4' in fifty years." It looks like 2015 may be the best, greatest vintage of them all. But they each have their own nuances and special charm.

A number of factors have contributed to the current success enjoyed by most Burgundian growers. Burgundian farmers have long been the avant garde as far as technical knowledge and innovation when it comes to growing grapes. Other areas of France, most notably Bordeaux, have learned from them and emulated their techniques. Conscientious growers do an incredible amount of vineyard work to reduce crop size, meaning yields, so as to grow the ripe, healthy grapes. Although weather has been warmer in Burgundy in recent years, there are always different weather-related exigencies that must be dealt with throughout the growing cycle. Relatively easy vintages with consistently good weather, like 2005, 2009, and 2015, which were easier to work and less taxing on the growers than most vintages, are rare. With extensive vineyard work using advanced viticultural techniques, high-quality, delicious wines were produced even in the most trying vintages.

While 2006, 2007, and 2008 were very difficult vintages for Burgundian growers, the four Burgundy vintages 2010, 2011, 2012, and 2013 were the most difficult yet, each with crops far below the norm. Then the Burgundians got hit with the most difficult climatically of all, 2016. Mother Nature threw the kitchen sink at them that vintage year. In the not-so-distant past those vintages would have been wipeouts, gone, disasters. In unprecedented fashion, 2010, 2011, 2012, and 2013 had adverse weather during the June/July flowering period. This resulted in poor grape set. Grape set is critical for wine production, as it determines the potential crop yield. In each of these past four vintages much of the crop was lost, as the vines had too many bunches of grapes that just dropped.

When there's loss of crop due to bad grape set, followed by uneven weather in August, that's a serious problem. When that happens four vintages in a row, that's a potential catastrophe. To exacerbate the situation in 2010, on December 19 and continuing until the next day, temperatures dropped from 40°F to below minus 10°F. This killed a number of vines, especially those very young and very old, mainly in less-exalted areas, but no commune was exempt. The Côte de Nuit alone suffered an estimated 100 hectares of lost vines! That's over 240 acres of the most expensive real estate imaginable, and it will take years for the growers to recover. So if you wonder why Burgundies cost what they do, here is another reason.

For these four vintages, and in 2016, conscientious growers were compelled to use many of the interventions and techniques that they had learned over the years to reduce yields by eliminating unsound grapes to ensure that nothing but perfect chardonnay and pinot noir grapes were harvested. Much vineyard work was needed to save these vintages and to allow good to great wine to be made. However, by doing this work and using these techniques, with no compromising on quality, they shot themselves in the foot financially, although there wasn't much wiggle room.

Viticultural Techniques

Listed below are the important viticultural steps used by the growers to insure quality, which has virtually eliminated any disastrous Burgundy vintages. But here's the rub: these steps dramatically increase the cost of production. Each of these extraordinary measures means more work, increased labor costs, and a much smaller production, regardless of vintage. Smaller production means less profit. Importers worry that some of the less-well-known Burgundian growers, as well as some with vineyards in less-famous Appellation d'Origine Contrôlée regions, will finally discontinue using these labor-intensive interventions if by such use they can't turn a profit. We fear that some of the lesser lights will feel forced to compromise on quality by using shortcuts. Unfortunately, however, there are no reliable shortcuts to quality. These viticultural techniques listed below need to be employed every year in some fashion or another if consistently high-quality grapes are to be grown. So we have a catch-22 situation. Cut the quality, I am not a buyer; charge me too much, and ditto, I can't sell your wine.

It seems as if the growers are between a rock and a hard place. Increasing production, thereby cutting the quality, is only a stop-gap measure financially, as the difference will surely be noticed in time. However, if the market will only pay X, regardless of uncompromised quality, and that amount won't cover costs, then what is the alternative? I know and do business with growers in this bind. Let me say this again: I would much rather be a wine merchant than a farmer.

1) In order to reduce yields and add power to their wine, growers debud in the spring. Debudding eliminates the shoots or sucker shoots that appear in the vine's trunk, as well as the spur shoots when these appear with more than a shoot per bud.

2) Green harvest (*vendange verte)* in June or July, depending on the vintage, is a relatively modern practice. Growers remove the tiny, immature grapes while they are still green, which induces the vine to put all its energy into developing the remaining grapes. This allows the grapes to ripen more evenly. We have fewer but healthier grapes, just bursting with juice and flavor, adding power to the wine.

3) In August they may have to deleaf if the weather is rainy or humid, whereby the leaves could spread humidity to the grapes

and thus increase the risks of rot. And at the end of August growers may cut from the vine any bunch of grapes that shows any signs of rot so there is no spread to other bunches.

4) Then during harvest they have the sorting tables, *les tables de trie*, where by hand they eliminate any grapes that aren't perfectly healthy.

These steps may be used, singly or all together, to give the grower/winemaker the ripest, healthiest grapes so that they can make the best wine possible. There is no set formula as to how the steps should be used, or not. Each grower has his or her own ideas.

In curtailed vintages 2010 through 2014, and especially in 2016, the growers had no way to give clients their usual expected annual allocations. And for most, there was no way for all but the most exalted estates to ask for prices close to what they needed to make a profit and stay solvent. Even with 10 to 25 percent price increases, there was no possibility that they could keep their books in the black. This was especially true for growers whose wines sell in the range of between ten and twenty-five euros per bottle, and even many who sell at thirty euros and above were in the same bind. Some, especially those in Beaune, which has been storm-ravaged for the past several years, were looking at potential financial ruin. Aubert de Villaine, of DRC fame, was quoted saying that for the 2012 vintage the growers were "at war" with nature to make the vintage a success. The year 2013 wasn't any easier, and 2016 was a nearly a wipeout for many vineyards. For those vintages the growers were able to produce only 50 percent or less of what they would in a normal year. When growers lose half their crop, mortgages still have to be paid, kids still need shoes and books. No, I do *not* want to be a farmer in Burgundy. Consecutive curtailed crops in vintages like 2010, 2011, 2012, and 2013 may have been unprecedented, but who is to say such vintages won't happen again? But, due to the effort of the beleaguered, hard-working vignerons, good to great wine was made in each of these four vintages. Even 2016 has its share of successes too.

We understand that the most sought-after Burgundies from the best-known villages and top domains will command high prices. However, high-quality Burgundy from great domaines, at prices under thirty dollars a bottle, even below twenty dollars, can be found with a little effort. It is possible for most wine lovers to experience Burgundy on many levels, if not the most exalted, without mortgaging the farm. Impeccably made Bourgogne Rouges and Blancs, 100 percent pinot noir for the red, 100 percent chardonnay for the white, from domaines like Anne Gros, Hudelot Noëllat, Digoia Royer, Albert Bichot, Paul Pernot, Henri Boillot, and many others are all often absolutely delicious. They mostly come from vineyards just outside of excellent villages and are very inexpensive for their pedigree and high quality. Also, the Côte Chalonnaise wines, both red and white, from Mercurey, Rully, and Givry are excellent values from many regional growers and shouldn't be missed. Less well-known villages such as Marsanny and Fixin in the Côte de Nuit, Monthelie, Santenay, Marange, and Chorey les Beaune from the Côte de Beaune offer excellent value also.

1er Crus and Grands Crus

Obviously, while 1er Cru and Grand Cru Burgundies, red and white, are no less affected by weather conditions than wines from lesser sites, they are at least bolstered by the excellent placement of their vineyard sites and the revenues gleaned from the sought-after wine they ultimately produce. The return these top producers get by maintaining quality and, therefore, the continued demand for their wines, sometimes regardless of the price, gives them the inspiration to do everything possible to make great wine. Of course, owners of these estates have the resources, meaning money, to do whatever it takes to produce their very low-production, high-quality wines. Hire a helicopter to dry the vineyards? If we have to, sure, bring it on. Smaller growers may well not be so fortunate. No helicopters for them.

Alsace

Alsace—A Great Place to Visit and Dine. Great Wines!

The capital of Alsace is Colmar, somewhat less than two hundred miles (three hundred km) from Beaune, which is in the heart of Burgundy. However, while French, Alsace shares a large border with Germany. Its inhabitants, understandably, have split personalities, as Germany annexed most of Alsace from France in 1871 after their victory in the Franco-Prussian War. The region has bounced back and forth between the two countries a number of times, but it is now decidedly French. I say that with some reservation because, as it extensively borders Germany, many if not most of the inhabitants retain some Germanic customs and habits not found in other parts of France. Their architecture is unique to France, unusual and quite remarkable, very Swiss/German.

The Alsatians tend to be far more like their German neighbors, former occupiers, than the rest of France. For example, they are decidedly more fastidious about general cleanliness and personal hygiene than is the French norm, which I heartily approve of. In many parts of France where grapes are grown it is not uncommon to see men, legs spread, straddling by the side of the road, unconcernedly adding their water to the vineyards. While this is more or less tolerated or ignored elsewhere and is not uncommon in Burgundy, it most certainly is not in Alsace. Try that there, and every car that passes will noisily and angrily honk their disapproval.

Alsace cuisine is far more in tune with Germany as well. Sausages, schnitzel, and other German fare not found elsewhere in France are more the norm than the exception. Lots of beer too, but they still do love their Alsace wine. And well they should, because even though most of their bottlings are confusingly similar to the tall, fluted German wine bottles, the wine contained therein is emphatically, defiantly French.

There are thousands of grapes grown in the world. Italy report-edly grows over three thousand varieties, but only a handful are con-strued as being "noble grapes." Cabernet sauvignon, merlot, pinot noir, chardonnay, and nebbiolo may come readily to mind for most of us. Riesling, which is also a noble grape, might not be thought of so easily or quickly, but should. Wine produced from high-quality Riesling grapes grown in Alsace can be racy, elegant, steely, complex, concentrated, and long-lived. The best can look wine from Burgundy, Bordeaux, or anywhere in the eye and not back down an inch, costing infinitely less. Those of us in the wine trade know well that often even Grand Cru Alsace wines can be found selling for a song on the wine lists of some of the best, most highly acclaimed restaurants around the world. The same can be true at retail.

I go to Alsace only sporadically now, but in the distant past I went there yearly. Taking the TGV, fast train, from Paris is easy. It takes under three hours from Paris and under two hours from Burgundy. I always wanted to go to the three-star restaurant Auberge de l'Ill in Illhaeusern. I heard so many wonderful things about it but was never able to secure a reservation. In the hopes of getting one due to a cancellation, Bonnie and I stayed two or three times at a hotel just on the edge of Illhaeusern called Hôtel La Clairière. Still in existence, it is a funny, funky kind of garish place but with large and comfortable rooms.

One time, after we had settled in, I went to the charming young concierge and asked her to inquire if there were any cancellations/reservations at Auberge de l'Ill. She said, "On ne sait jamais." You never know. But, alas, no luck this time. "Since you are interested in haute cuisine," she said, "may I recommend a restaurant that serves excellent food. It is called Jean-Frédéric Edel, in Sélestat. May I reserve for you?" Sure.

We headed off relatively early that evening, as we were travel weary. The restaurant, which happily still exists in Sélestat, a sort of unprepossessing village, was not very large but was beautifully appointed, with lots of beautiful hanging flowers outside. Inside, we were the first to arrive and had the restaurant to ourselves. That made me a bit nervous, but everything looked sparklingly clean, with more lovely flowers, and it had its own rustic charm. I ordered a bottle of Alsace riesling, I can't remember which one, and was ready to order dinner. The menu wasn't complex or complicated, which suited me fine that night. I ordered a simple salad and an order of pasta. My expectations weren't high, so I was shocked at the beautiful presentation of my salad, which was absolutely delicious, one of the best ever. My pasta dish, featuring cheese and leeks, was no less delightful. I loved the meal. No, we didn't get to go to a "three star," but we were more than happy with where we went and what we ordered.

Dinner at Au Crocodile—Strassburg

On one of our periodic excursions to Alsace, we had an appointment at the renowned Domaine Schlumberger, where we were met by the charming and elegant Evelyn Bedón (née Schlumberger). We had an interesting and informative, very enjoyable tasting with her, which took most of the morning. This was on a Thursday. Before we left, she asked how long we would be staying. "Until Monday," we responded. "Well then, you should really go to the wonderful three-star restaurant Le Crocodile in Strasbourg. I am friendly with the owner. Would you like me to make a reservation for you?" "Well, sure, that would be great," I said. "Saturday night would work for us, as we have no plans as yet." Evelyn assured us she would take care of it, and off we went without another thought.

We left a bit early Saturday so that we could be sure to find the restaurant easily and to allow some time to walk around the city. The day was somewhat overcast, threatening but not rainy. We found the city to be rather somber and somewhat ominous as well. There were a number of churches scattered throughout the city. We were admiring the angular, sharp-pointed Gothic architecture of one rather striking example when we realized that it was literally dwarfed and overshadowed by an even more striking, completely humongous church that had spirals reaching for the stars. I got a crick in my neck looking up at it. I said to Bonnie, "You know what this reminds me of? Remember when Sigourney Weaver in the movie *Aliens* went down to rescue the little girl, Rebecca, and she looked up and saw the huge, big mama egg-laying alien who dwarfed everything else?" No disrespect to the church, but that was the image I couldn't get out of my mind.

With a little research, I found out that the church was the Strasbourg Cathedral, or the Cathedral of Our Lady of Strasbourg. It is widely considered to be among the finest examples of high, or late, Gothic architecture, and it dates back to 1277. At 466 feet, it was the world's tallest building from 1647 to 1874, so there was a reason why I was craning my neck. Today it is the sixth-tallest church in the world and the highest extant structure built entirely in the Middle Ages.

It was soon time for us to go to dinner. The restaurant was surprisingly large, and the exterior beautifully exemplified the Alsace architecture we found in the various towns and villages. We walked into a large enclave and told the maître d' our name and that we had a reservation for dinner. He checked his book and, shaking his head, said, "C'etait pour hier soir." It was for yesterday evening. Unlike today, there were no calls in advance to confirm reservations and no demand for a credit-card number to keep on file in case one doesn't show up. I gently protested that, indeed, the reservation was for this evening and that Evelyn Bedón had made the reservation for us, personally.

We were really not overly upset, just somewhat frustrated. Mistakes occur, and it was obvious that this must have been a miscommunication. I knew we would find someplace nice to dine. While this not lengthy discussion was going on, a middle-aged lady came over and rather imperiously asked the maître d', "Qu'est-ce qui se passe ici?" What's going on here? There was no question that she was the owner of Le Crocodile, Madame Jung. She was maybe five feet one or two inches tall and was wearing a long, brocaded formal dress. After she received an explanation and checked the reservation herself, she turned to the maître d' and said, "Faites quelque chose." Do something! We were kindly asked to wait and, as the restaurant was, of course, fully booked, they had to get a table for us, which they set up in the aisle. We kind of stuck out, but who cared, we were seated and soon gave our order. The only food course I can recall was a slab of fois gras that melted in my mouth like chocolate. The wine, too, was most memorable that night. I felt compelled to order a Schlumberger wine. I would have been embarrassed not to.

My choice was their 1982 Grand Cru Riesling Kitterle. As I have noted, Grand Cru riesling, especially in Alsace, are often fabulous values, as was the case with this. The wine was crystalline, pure, mineral tinged, stylish, and concentrated. The balance was perfect, and anyone who thinks that all rieslings are sweet should have the luck to try a wine like this. It was crisp and poised, with obvious class and pedigree. It was so sharp and penetrating that, in a good way, it cut through our food like a scimitar. Domaine de Chevalier Blanc couldn't have been better. About midway through our meal Madame Jung stopped by to see how things were going. I told her how much we were enjoying everything and thanked her profusely for setting up the table and allowing us to stay. She looked me in the eye and said, in English, "We never do that." There is no question that thanks were due to Evelyn, or we would have missed a fabulous experience.

Auberge de l'Ill

September is a great time to go to Alsace, as the Vosge Mountains protect the area from inclement weather, and they often have some beautiful Indian summers. We did finally make it to Auberge de L'Ill one September. This time we stayed with them at their inn and therefore were able to make a dinner reservation. We went on a night when there was a fine mist in the air. Bonnie, as always was impeccably and stylishly dressed. I wore a suit. This was a three-star restaurant, after all, and was deserving of respect. One wonders what their dress code might be today.

Anyway, the dining room where we were to be seated was rectangular. We were escorted to the rear, where our table had side-by-side seating. It was a great table, and we could see the entire room, with a lovely view of the lake. Because of Bonnie's food allergies, the safest choice for her was that evening's special offering of a local river fish.

I don't remember the name, but know that it had to be ordered for two. I said, "Fine" and hoped for the best, as that would not have been my first choice. We started off, as was my wont in Alsace, with fois gras. It, too, was like melt-in-your-mouth chocolate. The river fish was the exact opposite of bland: it was flavorful and interesting and was beautifully presented. We loved it and the whole experience. Of course, I had a Grand Cru riesling with dinner, this time from Zind Humbrecht. That was the only time we ever went to Auberge de l'Ill; I wish that we might one day go back again.

Domaine Gerard Metz

Traveling with my friend, importer Jim Elston in March of 2014, we were very late for our scheduled visit to Domaine Metz, as one of our group of seven was delayed connecting with us. We had just flown into Paris from Boston and gotten on the first train available to Alsace when he texted to say that he would be late by at least a few hours. Great! Once we arrived after our two-hour train ride from Paris, we just hunkered down at the train station and waited for him. We finally ordered lunch at the station. I wasn't enticed by any of the offerings on the modest restaurant menu, so I—cleverly, it turned out—just ordered an omelet. The food was, to be kind, not good, but my omelet and the salad with it were fine. How was the wine we chose? Worse than the food. I ordered a beer; others decided to do likewise.

We were very relieved when our missing compatriot finally showed up. We had been concerned, and perturbed, as he was incommunicado for nearly three hours. It's a good thing we liked him so much, otherwise we may have cheerfully strangled him, verbally of course. Needless to say, we were very late getting to our hotel, and I was exhausted. Eric Casimir, who runs Domaine Metz, had dinner reservations for us at a very nice restaurant. Everyone went and had a great time, except me. I blew it off and went to my room, read for a while, and then crashed. This was the first day of a fourteen-day excursion, and I knew what to expect. This was not my first rodeo. That's right: the life of a wine merchant is *not* all fun and games.

The next day I was relatively chipper. Others looked a bit green around the gills, but everyone said going to the restaurant was worth it and that I had missed a good time. So be it. I didn't doubt them but had no regrets. We got to the winery around 9:30 a.m., and Eric showed us around. The winery is located in the pleasant, but somewhat drab, somewhat gloomy, village of Ittersville. The village is located halfway between Strasbourg and Colmar, on the eastern slope of the Vosges Mountains.

Eric Casimir is an interesting man. Tall, slim, maybe in his late thirties or early forties, he speaks excellent English, is very passionate about his work and his wines, and is articulate in expressing that passion. We knew to allow at least a few hours when tasting there, as Eric usually has many bottles from various sites and vintages to try, including some Grands Crus. He is quite content to talk about them and their differences at length and is a compelling advocate of his wines in particular and Alsace wines in general. The combination of Eric and his wines is most persuasive. If you don't fall in love with Metz wine after visiting, then you must not love wine.

Eric told us that the Metz estate was rather small, including only twelve hectares (around twenty-five acres) of vines, with vineyards that have diverse soil types. He explained that he runs the estate as organically as possible by the *lutte raisonnée* method. That means unless the crop is in jeopardy, he will not use nonorganic treatments.

We started tasting in his very nice *chais*, and the first wine was a sparkling Champagne lookalike, Crémant d'Alsace. We then segued into his rieslings and other varietals, including two excellent gewurztraminers. I very much liked his old-vine riesling, but his Cuvée Tradition line, made from younger vines on the estate (twenty to twenty-four years old), is delicious and is at an attractive price point. All the Metz wines are fresh, bright, refreshingly crisp, and varietally correct. The single-vineyard Grand Cru Münchberg is fabulous, with strong character, bracing minerality, and deep, complex flavors. The

Vieilles Vignes Riesling and Gewurztraminer VV are from thirty-to-eighty-year-old vines and show outstanding richness, complexity, texture, and length.

In general, the wines of this estate are finished dry and clean with plenty of ripe, fresh fruit balanced by crisp acidity. On the palate they have a fine, rich texture and great length from the extended lees contact. The basic typicity of each grape variety and soil type shines through clearly. As a group they are excellent examples of well-made wines that can be produced in Alsace at very reasonable prices for the quality.

What is ever so refreshing about Eric is that he takes no shortcuts in making his wine. Everything is done by hand: the work in the vineyards, the picking at harvest, and the bottling. He personally oversees everything.

I may have missed dinner the previous night with the group, but I was certainly ready for lunch on this day. Eric took us to a local restaurant, a large, bustling, unadorned place that was full of people and crackling with energy. He chose it for us so as to expedite our time, as we had many miles to go. He had been kind enough to order ahead for us, family style. Let me say this up front. When I am in France on business, I eat in a completely different manner than when I am at home. Generally, I almost never eat lunch. In France on business, it is a must. After tasting all morning, even with spitting and not swallowing wine, the acids in your stomach need to be absorbed, so lunch, with as much fat as possible, is required. Of course, I shun fat too when not on the road. And I invariably am forced to eat food that I would not even consider having when at home, sometimes to my detriment. I have learned the hard way not to eat the same things, or at least not the same quantities, as the English expats with whom I work, or I may well wish I were dead. Those English, bless 'em, have cast-iron stomachs and could eat the horns off a goat. I have also learned not to drink with my French colleagues or they will lose me, and possibly leave me, under the table.

To get back to lunch with Eric: We were offered two main

courses served family style, one a platter of sweetbreads and one of tripe, both in some kind of cream sauce. Did I mention that at home I avoid cream sauces? And tripe? No way. Well, I was there, and I hadn't had dinner the night before and was hungry, so in I dug. One of the members of our group blanched at these two offerings and asked if he could order a steak. I almost followed suit but persevered. I must say, the food was abundant and tasty, real rustic home-style Alsatian food and served with terrific *frites*, French fries, as well. Thankfully, I had no ill effects.

The unexpected highlight of the meal for me were two bottles of 2011 Michel Noëllat Nuits Saint Georges that Eric plunked down on the table next to his wines. I was intrigued, as I do business with Hudelot-Noëllat, distant cousins it turns out, and I love red Burgundy. The wine went great with the heavy, rustic food, and the crisp acids of the young Nuits Saint Georges cut right through the sauce and possibly saved me to live to see another day. I noted the address of the domaine and when we got to Burgundy, later in the trip, made sure we paid the Michel Noëllat domaine a visit. I have been buying their wine ever since, thanks to Eric. I was not disappointed to have missed dinner the previous evening but would have been very sorry not to have been there for the lunch.

An Alsace Misadventure

One of the Alsace producers I did business with when I first started my importing company made wines we adored. They were crisp, stylish, sharply delineated, and distinctive. They also offered a Grand Cru riesling that had precise character and a soulful personality and sold for a song. Even though the market for Alsace wines was even worse then than now, we did reasonable business with his wines for more than a few years.

Then one day we showed up at his hard-to-find *chais* and started our tasting. Uh oh, something had changed. The varietal character was muted. The wines, all of them, tasted off, as if something was masking or blocking the true, expected flavors. Was that grass I tasted?

This was a very proud man, so we had to be somewhat circumspect in asking, "What did you do differently this year? The wines seem to have changed." This is an old, sad story, so you have probably have heard it before. With a large grin, he directed us outside to proudly show us this huge machine he had bought to do the picking, saving on hiring human pickers. He thought it was great to be unburdened by them. We were horrified. My colleague and I looked at each other wide-eyed. We thanked him for the tasting and left for the first time without placing an order. Once in the car, we looked at each other and proclaimed that the problem with his wine was the "*gout de la machine.*" The taste of the machine, which could not avoid weak or rotten bunches and, blindly, would add extraneous bits that a human picker would have eliminated. I checked this grower out online, and he seems to be getting good reviews, so I will not do him the disservice of mentioning his name. But having been "snake-bit" once, I can't bring myself to ever buy his wines again. I know what they were, shining with pristine purity that for me was forever tarnished by the *gout de la machine*. I don't want to know how they taste today.

Southern Rhône

Domaine Font de Michelle

I have been importing wines from Domaine Font de Michelle for over twenty years and have always loved their style of Châteauneuf du Pape. There is an elegance and finesse to their wines every vintage that is not found in other Châteauneufs. They have a silky, Burgundian feel, probably due to the high amount of grenache, around 75 percent, used in their regular bottling. Their special cuvée, Etienne Gonnet, named after their founder, is deeper, as it contains a higher percentage of syrah and comes from older, well-placed vines. It, too, has a remarkable Burgundian silkiness that makes it deliciously irresistible almost as soon as it is released, but is still a wine that can age and develop beautifully over time. Font de Michelle also makes a very small amount of Châteauneuf du Pape called Elegance de Jeanne, which is made from 100 percent grenache grapes from 110-year-old vines. Yummy stuff but rare.

The Gonnet family has been in the southern French town of Bédarrides since the early 1600s. Etienne Gonnet created Domaine Font de Michelle in 1950. They have thirty hectares of contiguous vineyard space authorized to make appellation Châteauneuf du Pape. The fact that they are all connected in one lot is unusual for Châteauneuf, as most often plots are separated and scattered. Their vineyard has perfect placement for sun exposure, as it is in the southeastern part of the Châteauneuf du Pape AOC. It is located not far from those of their relatives, the Bruniers, at Vieux Telegraphe, although Font de Michelle's style of Châteauneuf differs somewhat from theirs.

Etienne's, sons, Jean and Michel, also known as Bruno, have run the estate since 1975. They constantly strive to make great wine every year, wines that are concentrated and elegant, yet fairly priced for this super-heated appellation. Recently, they have passed the baton to their sons, Bertrand and Guillaume, who have added twenty hectares of Côtes du Rhône and Côtes du Rhône Village from the village of Signargues. These, too, offer the elegant style and pedigree of the Estate.

Jean and Bruno are big guys, Bruno especially. Jean is taller but Bruno, while giving up some height, is more compact and is heavily muscled. He is, or was, very athletic and goes in for mountain climbing. That for me would be a spectator sport, thank you. They are, however, gentle giants. Their cave where the wines are kept in cask is rather deep with steep steps. One spring morning when I was visiting, we headed down to the cave with Jean, who is far more long legged than I. He was practically running. Foolishly, forgetting my age, I tried to keep up with him and tripped, striking my knee on the stone floor rather forcefully "Ça va?" he asked. Are you all right? Of course I said, "Yes." But I was lying. After the tasting, the colleague with whom I was traveling asked me the same question as I limped to the car. "Not really," I replied. "I can't bend my leg." It was a good thing he was driving. Our next stop was to one of my favorite Côtes du Rhône producers, Château Courac, which was not that far away in the tiny village of Laudon. Owners Joséphine and Frédéric Arnaud have a lovely home that looks out over the vineyards. Joséphine, who is small, dark, and birdlike but wiry, is of Sicilian descent. Frédéric is medium sized, heavyset, and strong, with a full, pleasant, open face. They make a full range of Côtes du Rhône, but for me, the star of the show every year is their Côtes du Rhône Villages-Laudon, produced from grapes grown on their own vineyards.

When I arrived, it was quite obvious that I was in pain. Joséphine said that she had some medicine that I should rub into my knee. I said, "No thank you. May I have some ice instead?" So while we had our tasting with bottles Frédéric had previously prepared and placed on their kitchen table, I iced up and started to loosen up. Joséphine, ever the caring hostess, offered to make us lunch with some aspara-gus that they had just picked from their own garden. I have to admit, I am not a big asparagus fan, as it is not wine friendly. But we said yes anyhow. Joséphine served them up with some homemade aioli and fresh bread. I couldn't get enough of them. Did they go with the wine? Who cared, we drank it anyhow.

That night I skipped dinner, not usual, as dinner is often our treat after a long day of tasting. I stayed in my room and iced my knee all night long. The next day, magically, it was if I had never fallen.

Gasoil Is French for Diesel Fuel?

This incident happened over twenty-five years ago. For at least ten years afterward, I wouldn't even talk about it. Four of us were traveling to diverse regions of France looking for new producers who were making good, affordable wine. I was there strictly as a retailer, as it hadn't yet entered my mind to become a wine importer. Our group consisted of me, the owner and general manager of a small, quality-oriented import company with whom I did a lot of business, and a wine-store manager/buyer from the western part of Massachusetts. We were in two cars, as we often split up to cover more ground.

A few days into the trip, I felt obliged to change dollars into francs. Why? No clue, as I am sure I had a credit card. We decided we would split up, with me and the retailer, Paul, going to the bank to exchange currency. The other two were supposed to check out a prospective supplier in Châteauneuf du Pape, which was not too far away. We agreed to meet at the entrance to the autoroute and continue on together. After the money exchange, I realized that the gas tank of the car, a lovely, sexy, nimble, and quick Lancia, was only one-third full. Wanting to be a nice guy and save time, I decided to fill it up. This was a mistake of gigantic proportions. I pulled up to the pump and although I knew that in French "gas" is called *essence*, I stopped in front of a pump marked *gasoil* and filled the car up.

Stop. Don't laugh. Believe me, I was not the first person to do this, nor was I to be the last, and some of them were French. I mean, OK. *Gasoil*. Cars need gas and oil, right? So who knew that for the French *gasoil* meant diesel fuel? Can a gasoline car run on diesel fuel? After a few miles, when the car started bucking and dark black smoke began farting out of the rear, I found out that, no, they can't. We just made it to the beginning of the autoroute when my little Italian beauty sighed her last sigh and gave up the ghost. Can anyone say Murphy's Law?

Since we were at the beginning of the autoroute where we were supposed to soon meet our friends anyway, we should have been OK, right? Not really. I had missed the first sign for the autoroute, which was to the left, just outside the bank. I headed for the next (wrong) autoroute exit, three to four miles away. No cell phones, no way to communicate with the rest of our party, and certainly no AAA. After an hour of just sitting there I got fidgety, and since I spoke some French and had our itinerary, I decided to try to call M. Jean Lionnet in Cornas, our next scheduled stop. I had to cross over the Route National to get to a gas station and then navigate the pay phone. M. Lionnet answered, and I explained our situation and asked him to tell our friends that we were looking for them and to come get us. Unbeknownst to us and them, we were at the wrong autoroute exit. They went to the exit closest to the bank, never saw us, and assumed we were doing our own thing. To compound matters, they then decided to skip Cornas and continue on. Not a helpful decision.

You must be wondering what my passenger, Paul, was doing throughout all of this. Absolutely nothing. He was as stoic and helpful as a wooden Indian. He hardly moved and said not a word. I guess I should have been grateful. If I were in his shoes I may well have cussed me out. I know I was not happy with myself. Another hour went by. No one showed. I crossed the street again and called M. Lionnet once more. "No, they haven't arrived, and I have received no word from them," he said. "Would you like me to come and get you?" Yes, please.

He showed up in some ancient little old French car, took us back to his place in Cornas, and made arrangements to have the Lancia towed and the gas tank etc. cleaned out so that the beautiful little car would once again be operational. By the way, entering the town of Cornas was like being in a time warp back to the '30s. I had never seen anything like it. Finally, after many hours, the other two hooked up with us. They were pissed at us, me, for blowing their schedule. It's true that I did mess things up, as time is precious on these trips. And I was beyond furious, because they never made an effort to find out what happened to us. Wine merchants, and others, do have accidents. One might have assumed some caring or worry on their part when they lost us and/or maybe even some compassionate humor once they learned what had occurred. Nada. We all went to bed angry. Growers in Crozes Hermitage were scheduled to be seen the next day. I couldn't have cared less and was planning not to go. Paris, here I come.

Before climbing into bed, I heard a knock on my door. My colleague/friend, owner of the import company, was standing there and said, "I know you are upset and intend to leave the trip tomorrow. Please don't. We still have lots of great wines to try, and we would miss having you." I looked at him, thought for a minute or two, and said, "Yeah, OK. I'm still in." It didn't take much to mollify me. That doesn't mean I was happy.

The next day we drove in our two cars to Crozes Hermitage. Yes, I was the Lancia's driver. After spending over one hundred dollars to have the gas tank emptied and cleaned out and the engine treated, I expected the Lancia to be as good as new. Not even close. There was still some, probably never to be gotten rid of, residue of diesel fuel in the system, and she still occasionally bucked and backfired, polluting the area with not-pleasant-smelling black smoke. Crozes Hermitage was rustic but seemed a thriving, modern metropolis after Cornas. They definitely didn't deserve the gas attack we gave them. We tried some wine with two or three growers. Nothing of great interest, however.

It was later in the afternoon after a day of sampling that Paul, previously borderline comatose, made this startling observation. "Look at the Lancia's trunk," he said. "You know, I have been looking at the trunk for a couple of days now and have noticed that it doesn't quite latch all the way." Yes, so? "Well, if it isn't connecting, then maybe it's wearing down the battery." So now he tells us. And guess what?

Sure enough, he was right. The car wouldn't start, and we had to call a service for a jumpstart. Talk about being snakebit.

This, too, held us up, as we wanted to get back to Avignon, a trip of around an hour and a half, so we could catch a train to Burgundy. Would we make it? After the mechanic got the car going, pocketing lots of francs, he admonished us to keep it running because if it stalled again it might not start. Great. We started a two-car convoy back to Avignon, Paul and me in the Lancia. You-know-who driving. There was no autoroute back to Avignon then, so we had to go by *routes nationals*. There were stoplights and traffic. I pretty much kept up to our second car, but only by keeping the Lancia revved to the max. When we stopped at a stoplight I pushed in the clutch and kept it wound at three thousand rpm. All the way to Avignon I don't think I ever shifted into fourth. Second and third were as far as I dared to go. This was a sweat-inducing, hair-raising ride; I knew that if that car stalled, we were on our own.

We finally made into Avignon and, breathing hard, I parked in front of the car-rental agency. As soon as I put it in neutral and took my foot off the gas, the car stalled and would not start. *Finito la musica*. That's the end of that. We were glad to have made it safely back to Avignon and to be shut of the Lancia. But the guilty feelings I had about what I did to that splendid little car persist to this day.

Rhône Vintages

We, in the US, are so "vintage conscious" that we sometimes lose sight of the fact that every year is a vintage year, each with its own unique style and personality. Not all Bordeaux can be 1982s, 1990s, or 2000s, nor should they be. And not all Côtes du Rhône can be or should be 2007s or 2010s. It's not possible and, anyway, each should be enjoyed for its own individual qualities and characteristics.

The 2011 and 2012 southern Rhônes, including Châteauneuf du Pape, Gigondas, Vacqueyras, and Côtes du Rhône Villages are totally delicious in a more Burgundian style than we would normally expect.

Most of the wines are balanced, fresh, and supple, with gorgeous aromatics and silky, supple tannins. One would have to go back to the vastly underrated 2006 vintage to find wines with more stunning bouquets.

The southern Rhône has been blessed over the years with consistently excellent vintages, with more than a few great. Only 2002 and 2008 out of the past fifteen vintages have had wines that suffered qualitatively due to adverse weather conditions. Though 2011 was not considered a blockbuster southern Rhône vintage like 2010, 2007, or 2005, what it does offer, generally, is a wonderfully balanced style that is totally and immediately delicious. There is slightly lower alcohol than we have seen recently, and that's not a bad thing. Wines of 14 to 15 percent or more can overwhelm the palate, as can excessive tannins. The 2011s seem to have more terroir typicity and transparency than in other years. The 2012s and 2014s are not dissimilar but seem to have a bit more stuffing than the 2011s, with many wines rated well into the 90s by various wine writers. The 2015s, both north and south, are great.

While in Burgundy a few Septembers ago, a colleague and I stayed at my *auberge* of preference, the delightful La Chouette in Puligny, across the street from the well-known inn Le Montrachet. Suzanne, the owner, whom I have known for years, provided us with a lovely home-cooked dinner, and we always bring in thirty to forty or so wines to try with our meal each night. This is very efficient and more relaxing than trying to get the work done at a restaurant. On the second evening we had, among quite a few others, a bottle of 2008 Nuits Saint George 1er Cru Les Murgers from a famous producer, graciously given to us by the winemaker. It was a terrific albeit young wine with more pedigree than anything we had on the table. But it has to be admitted, the wine we loved the most that night and kept going back to was the 2011 Châteauneuf du Pape from Font de Michelle. Its lively, racy fruit flavors and supple elegance made it our wine of the night. Many 2011and 2012 Rhônes are like that, too, and deserve recognition.

If you were to suggest to the vignerons that the 2011 or 2012 vintage is less good than 2010, they will stare at you in perturbed disbelief. While they concede that 2010 will live longer, most, I believe correctly, consider 2011 and 2012 terrific, very successful years with delicious wines. Most growers sold off their 2010s, as it was the "hot," more acclaimed vintage, and will drink 2011s and 2012s.

I understand their mentality, as I have sold almost all the most sought-after 2005, 2009, and 2010 Burgundies that I could get. I did keep some, of course, but have cellared personally, quite happily thank you, select 2006s, 2007s, 2008s, and 2011s. This is analogous to what many Rhône growers have done, or are doing, with their 2011s and 2012s. Those Burgundy "off" vintages cost less than those that are more exalted by the wine press but, when well chosen from the best producers, are often excellent. Many 2006 Burgundy reds are drinking well now, the better 2007s, especially Chambolles, have been beautiful for a while, and the 2008s could be left alone for a year or so to resolve their tannins. I find many 2011 and 2012 Burgs seductive and irresistible, just bursting with fruit. Of course, as of this writing, the 2014s are showing beautifully.

Château Rayas—Châteauneuf du Pape

Visiting and tasting with Jacques Reynaud at Château Rayas, thirty or so years ago, was always one of the highlights of my trip. It wasn't that Reynaud was so personable. He wasn't. Or that the property was pristine. It was just the opposite, with goats and young goatherders wandering around in a seemingly aimless fashion. I loved going there because of the very educational tastings of great wines that M. Reynaud conducted in his cave.

At the time, Jacques Reynaud must have been close to seventy years of age, or at least he looked it. He was very short, maybe five feet two or three inches tall, a bit paunchy, with an incongruous (as it turns out) cherubic, pixie aspect to his face. He was actually very sly (*il était rusé*), and while he never was what I would call voluble, he loved to test tasters. He would try us on various *cuvées*, wines aging in different barrels, asking us to guess what grape varieties were in each barrel. He would twist his head to one side and regard us quizzically while waiting for a response. Although Château Rayas purportedly was always 100 percent old-vine grenache, he also had old-vine plantings of mourvedre, carignan, and syrah, as well as grenache. I can't tell you that I ever guessed which was which correctly, or that any of my traveling companions did either, but the amazing intensity of the flavors—I can taste them still—were so pronounced and deep that although I had no clue what we were trying, I really didn't care. I can say, unequivocally, they were all unique and fabulous. He could have bottled any one of them singly, and it would have been a great wine.

The fact is, Reynaud was a master blender and, in his case, that is an understatement of huge proportions. Yes, Rayas was 100 percent grenache, made up of select barrels to go into the final blend, but Château Pignan, also a Châteauneuf du Pape, and the Côtes du Rhône, Château Fonsalette, could be made up of various grape variety blends. Reynaud also occasionally made a Château Fonsalette Cuvée Syrah Pure, which was 100 percent syrah, but I will come back to that. We once asked him how he learned to become such a remarkable blender. He claimed that he learned the craft from his father and that his sister, who also lived on the property, was as accomplished at it as he.

Château Rayas wasn't initially as in demand back then as it became in the late '90s and beyond. In 1985 I was offered a great deal on some 1979 Château Rayas, supposedly not a great Châteauneuf du Pape vintage. It was retailing then for under $20 a bottle. I loved it, and for my wife's fortieth birthday party that was the red wine I served to our guests; it was super at six years of age.

I also offered my retail customers an amazing deal on 1990 Château Rayas when it was first released. Buy one case each of 1990 Rayas, one of 1990 Pignan, and one of 1990 Fonsalette for $999.99. I just looked online, and the average price for one bottle of 1990 Château Rayas today is $1,600! I told my customers at the time that by buying a case of Rayas and Pignan, they would be getting a case of Château Fonsalette for free. I didn't have any idea of how truly I spoke.

I never took home any Château Rayas 1990, nor did I cleverly set any aside. The 1990 Château Pignan, which reputedly is the second wine of Rayas and from the Rayas property, was nearly as good as Rayas itself. One would have had a tough time telling the difference between the two back then, and Pignan was much less expensive. While the 1990 Pignan may not have been 100 percent grenache, as was Rayas, whatever was in the blend was fabulous. I took a couple of cases of that home for myself and also loaded up, again personally, with Château Fonsalette and Château Fonsalette Côtes du Rhône Syrah Pure. There were very few Châteauneuf du Papes, then or now, that could be anywhere near as good as those wines.

I mentioned that there was disarray around the property. That confusion sometimes was extended to the *chais,* where the barrels were kept. After visiting, we would often buy some of the bottled wines to take with us, usually the Côtes du Rhône Château Fonsalette. That was because it was the one wine most likely to be available, and it always was far better than the price. When we finally opened a bottle of the Côtes du Rhône we bought at the estate, a good percentage of the time we would discover that we had Fonsalette Côtes du Rhône Cuvée Syrah Pure, instead of the regular bottling that we had ordered. We just assumed that either it didn't matter to Reynaud what we were given or that care wasn't taken labeling the wine for us, if it was labeled at all. Bottles in most cellars remain unlabeled (*déshabillé,* undressed) until an order is placed, as the labels would soon peel off due to the humidity. As one would assume, Cuvée Syrah Pure, with 100 percent old-vines syrah, was more expensive than the regular bottling, so we never complained.

I didn't really give it much thought but was reminded of it at dinner with Peter Vezan and his wife, Evelyne. We were at Taillevent and were somewhat daunted by the prices on the wine list, as we were not into spending megabucks on wine. We had just come back from Burgundy and could still mentally taste some of the great wines we had tried. I spotted a 1983 Côtes du Rhône Château Fonsalette on the list, a wine with which we were both abundantly familiar, and I said, "Let's get that." The bottle was terrific, bigger and more powerful than either of us remembered. We ordered another bottle. Unfortunately, it was corked. We sent it back and said to the sommelier, "Let's try again, and get the same wine." Just because one bottle is corked, that doesn't mean other wines in the case will be so afflicted. The next bottle was perfect and delicious. Peter and I looked at each other, shook our heads, and started laughing. *This* was the regular bottling. The first bottle was Cuvée Syrah Pure. Reynaud even goofed on his orders for temples of gastronomy like Taillevent. Amazing!

There was a good reason for the special success of the property back then. Rayas had naturally low yields, and Reynaud was always one of the last to pick grapes, as he was looking for maximum ripeness. He usually gambled and won. Their fifty-five acres of vineyards are divided into fifteen separate and distinct parcels with a terroir of rather poor, red, sandy soils, unusual for the region. These include a bit of limestone and clay with remarkably few stones, not the norm for Châteauneuf du Pape. The fact that the vines have to fight through the poor soils gives power to the grapes and adds character to the wine. There is also an interesting theory that the large pine and oak trees in their vineyards alter the microclimate of Château Rayas and thus the power and flavors of the wine.

Unfortunately, after Jacques Reynaud died in 1997, the quality of the wines went south, fast. His cousin Emmanuel Reynaud, who made Côtes du Rhône and Vacqueyras at his own property, Château des Tours, took over management of the estate. It is probably unfair to put all the blame for the diminished quality on Emmanuel's shoulders. No one could do with Rayas what Jacques Reynaud did. But, frankly, I was never a fan of Château des Tours' wines, so I was not sanguine about the future of Rayas after Jacque Reynaud's passing. Some of the old vines needed replacing before and after his death, and I understand that has been dealt with. They should be able to produce improved wines now. I am told they are better, although I haven't tasted any recent vintages. Reportedly, Emmanuel's son,

Louis Damien Reynaud, will be running the estate in the future. We will have to see what he can do, with fingers crossed. This is a legendary property that should be capable of offering some of the best wine in the world. That's what it did under enigmatic, iconoclastic, very strange Jacques Reynaud. Let's hope it will one day again.

Vacqueyras/Gigondas—Domaine Clos des Cazaux—Jean Michel Vache

Jean Michel Vache is one of my favorite growers. He and his very nice brother, Frédéric, have been in charge of their forty-eight-hectare property for over twenty years. The property, which dates back five generations, consists of twenty-four hectares in Vacqueyras and twenty hectares in Gigondas.

Jean Mich, as he is called, is of medium height and stocky, with a florid open face, piercingly intelligent eyes, and flashing smile. He is quick, energetic, bright, and more than occasionally funny. Just don't discuss politics with him. He is very opinionated, and he will never stop talking. I enjoy visiting the estate and tasting through his current vintages while listening to Jean Mich expound about various problems besetting a vigneron in his neck of the woods. He, like most vignerons I do business with, is overwhelmed by the amount of bureaucratic paperwork he is required to deal with. He would much rather spend time in the fields than in the office, but there is no way to get around it. The French government is very organized and has a slew of bureaucrats at the ready to cause grief to men like Jean Michel.

Unfortunately for them, but fortunately for us, Vacqueyras has less renown than Gigondas, and neither of them have the cachet of Châteauneuf du Pape. That is despite the fact that several domains in the region make wine that can compete with Châteauneuf du Pape. There are some that are their equal, or better, costing far less as well. Clos des Cazaux's Gigondas and Vacqueyras vineyards are located on steep, stony slopes, and the area can be rather arid. The vineyards are encircled by the beautiful mountainous range the Dentelles de Mont-mirail. Their very rich soil and optimal sun exposure give strength to the grape varieties, syrah, mourvedre, and grenache. All the grapes are handpicked and are traditionally vinified. Jean Mich keeps his wines in cask longer and releases them later than most of the other surrounding vineyards, and the difference shows.

I love the Clos des Cazaux wines—Vacqueyras Rouge Cuvée des Templiers and Gigondas Rouge Cuvée de la Tour Sarrasine especially. There are a few other Vacqueyras Cuvées produced at the domaine, but I always opt for the powerful yet elegant Cuvée des Templiers, which is made from nearly 100 percent old-vines syrah. Clos des Cazaux also offers a Gigondas Rouge Prestige that has wowed various wine writers, but I have always been perfectly happy with the elegant and rich regular Gigondas bottling. I have had ten- and twelve-year-old examples of it, and the wine has always remained fresh and surprisingly youthful. Jean Michel produces it from a blend of handpicked grapes: grenache, mourvedre, and old-vines syrah. When young, vibrant, and delicious, it has a deep, saturated ruby/purple color, excellent balance and structure, with well-integrated tannins. It becomes deeper and more complex with age. I wish I still had some of their 2007, which was wonderful. This Gigondas always features lots of pure, sensual, tasty/spicy *garrigue*-tinged flavors, usually with hints of blackberries and sandalwood. I find it has sneaky, understated power, with more elegance and complexity than one would expect. The Vacqueyras Rouge Cuvée des Templiers appears to be bigger due to the additional syrah, but the Gigondas can prove to be deceptively powerful. Again, I love them both differently. The domain often produces a small amount of a late-picked killer desert wine called Les Grains de Novembre that usually is not for export, as so little is made. It is fun to taste at the domaine.

There was a time when I was less than happy to see Jean Mich. I had just flown into Paris and taken the TGV to Avignon with no breaks and zero sleep. I can't sleep on planes or trains. In the past, on a business trip when I was young(er), I always flew directly from Boston to Paris's Charles de Gaulle Airport where, within an hour or so, I could take the train for Avignon when working first in the south. With no break and no sleep, I immediately began seeing my Châteauneuf du Pape and Rhône growers once I arrived, twenty-four hours after having left Boston. The folly of youth! This time, as usual, I arrived around midday and had no time for lunch, forget sleep. I was working with a longtime associate/colleague, an expat Englishman, Charles, who lives just outside Avignon. After he picked me up at the train station we went right out to see the growers. By the time we got back to his home around 7:30 p.m. or so, I was running on fumes.

Since I was staying with Charles that night, his charming wife was preparing a meal for us. Unbeknownst to me, Jean Michel was to be a guest. There was no place to run, no place to hide. I just wanted to eat and go to sleep. Jean Mich arrived around eight thirty. He was personable and voluble as always; however, dinner dragged interminably for me. While I speak fluent French, the subject matter and rapid-fire interplay was a bit much for me to follow, especially in my present state. I just sat there as if at a tennis match. I just wanted to go to bed! Finally, around midnight dinner was over, dishes were in the sink, and there was a decided lull in the conversation. I said to myself, "This is finally it. He is going to leave, and I can go to sleep." Not so fast. Unbelievably, Jean Mich looked at our host and sweetly asked, "Do you have any Scotch?" I mentally threw my hands up in the air and politely excused myself from the table and went up to bed.

Côtes du Rhône—Villages Cairanne— Domaine de l'Ameillaud

Cairanne, the Côtes du Rhône village that is home to Domaine de l'Ameillaud, is conveniently located thirty miles from Avignon and only forty miles from the lovely Côtes de Luberon village of Ménerbes, where we have spent some time in the past. There are quite a few wineries and charming villages that are fun to visit in the general area. They are all within easy striking distance of Cairanne, which makes it a great vacation spot. In fact, the owners, expatriate Englishman Nick Thompson and his French wife, Sabine, have some very nice, relatively recently built apartments available to rent out. Staying there would be a lot of fun for visitors, especially in the summer, as they even have a nice swimming pool just outside the vineyards. But that is not their principal source of income or the chief attraction.

Wine is the main reason for Domaine de l`Ameillaud's importance, as the winemaking history there goes back over two hundred years. Legend has it that Nick had an uncle who was an MW (master of wine), and it was he who inoculated Nick with the wine bug. When Nick met Sabine and fell in love, he was overjoyed to find out that her grandfather had property in Cairanne and was a grape grower. After their marriage, they visited the domaine, fell in love with it, and soon moved there. They both took courses at the wine school in Beaune. When they completed their studies, Granddad, who was getting long in the tooth, asked them if they wanted to manage the domain. The answer was a resounding, "Definitely yes, thank you sir, wow." That was in 1983, and they have been living and working there ever since. After Granddad passed away in 1991, they purchased a significant portion of the domain from his heirs.

The property encompasses around 140 acres (55 hectares), of which 90 acres lie in the AOC zone where Côtes du Rhône Villages Cairanne and generic Côtes du Rhône are produced. The remaining fifty acres produce an excellent Vin de Pays that is very close in quality to Côtes du Rhône but costs far less. Matt Kramer, in *Wine Spectator*, once wrote ecstatically about the qualities and very low price of this VDP. Matt was right, it is a wonderful value and would make a good choice as house wine.

Nick is a tall, slim, deceptively strong, jug-eared man who is maybe in his midfifties. When I visit him, since he is English, I get a respite from speaking French, which is sometimes welcome.

I have known him for many years and have great respect for him, his work ethic, which is amazing, and his wine, which I adore. Full-bodied, rich, powerful, and long lived, his Cairanne Côtes du

Rhône Village is always one of the best Côtes du Rhône bargains every year. Nick does much of the work himself, in the vineyard as well as in the *chais*. One year he did overstep himself and got in a bind. He had two tractor men working the vineyards. One of them came to him and demanded more money. Nick told him no, figuring that he and the other fellow could get all the work done. Then the other tractor driver had an accident and couldn't work. Nick was stuck doing it all by himself. "I was doing all right," he told me, "until August, when I got hit with unusual weather." He couldn't get to it all and ended up losing part of the crop. Oh well, live and learn. His is not an easy life, and he just squeaks by, but he loves it—at least most of it.

Southern French Wine

I love the wines from the beautiful, *garrigue*-scented, sun-drenched areas of Southern France. They are rich, alive, and full of vibrant flavors, individuality, and personality. The red grape varieties are primarily grenache, cinsault, mourvedre, and syrah, along with increasing amounts of cabernet sauvignon and merlot. Chardonnay and sauvignon blanc as well as other grape varieties such as viognier and grenache blanc may be included in the whites. The warm weather down south usually means that most Provençal wineries are able to harvest before the autumnal rains, and they are therefore generally less vulnerable to the potentially nasty late September/October weather that often afflicts areas not so climatically blessed.

There is literally a sea of soulful, spicy, full-bodied, relatively inexpensive/high-quality red wines produced in the Côtes du Rhône, Languedoc/Roussillon, Corbieres, Minervois, Côtes du Thongue, Baux en Provence, and Bandol. In the distant past, Southern French wines were considered, often correctly, undistinguished, rustic, and anonymous. For the past twenty or more years, that would not be true, especially since many younger, well-educated grower/winemakers have taken over their family's business.

Many of the wines offered on today's market from the above-mentioned regions are produced by small, individually owned estates. Their hands-on proprietors respect tradition yet employ sophisticated winemaking techniques and modern equipment. Most have reduced yields significantly to maximize quality. Generally, when we think of southern French wines we focus on the rich red wines like Châteauneuf du Pape or Gigondas for which they have become famous, but diverse, excellent dry rosés abound, and there are increasing quantities of cleanly made, good-quality whites. Prices remain fair and affordable. In spite of intense competition from Australia, South Africa, Spain, Portugal, and Italy, price to quality, many wines from Southern France still provide the quality yardstick against which all others should be measured.

Lunch with Lulu Peyraud at Domaine Tempier

When Kermit Lynch's book *Adventures on the Wine Route* was released in 1988 it was an instant success. It was especially appreciated by those of us in the trade and, more particularly, aspiring wine merchant/importers. I was and am a fan. Kermit is a great writer as well as a great wine importer. When the book first came out, *Wine Spectator* ran an honest, positive critique. One of their subscribers wrote in vehemently disagreeing with their assessment of the book, taking Lynch to task for, of all things, writing about wines that he imports. I wrote a letter to *Wine Spectator* defending Lynch and his book. "What would one want him to write about?" I asked. These were the wines and producers he knew best.

This was the first letter I had ever written to any publication, and to my surprise, it was published. One day I answered the phone at the shop, and the person on the other end asked, "Joel Berman?" "Speaking," I replied. "Kermit Lynch here" was the response. He thanked me for my letter in an amused, warm way, and we chatted for a while. When he came to Boston for a tasting some time later, we got together. We never became buddies—we are on either different coasts or different continents—but there was mutual professional respect and many common interests.

In the book, Kermit wrote glowingly about the Peyraud family in Bandol and about what a great, legendary cook Lulu Peyraud was, *patrone de* Tempier. If you go to the Tempier website now, there are some of Lulu's recipes listed. My wife, Bonnie, and I had planned a trip to France, so I called Kermit and asked if he could get us a tasting and luncheon date at the domaine. He did get us an invitation, and we went with great anticipation. We arrived midmorning on a perfect, cloudless, sun-blasted Provençal day. There was a young, midtwenties American couple visiting as well. They were from California and looked it: well built, robust, healthy, and full of energy. When we went to taste in the Tempier cave, the young lady declined and wandered around the property.

After tasting, we went in for lunch. The first hors d'oeuvres served were cheese balls made with Roquefort cheese. Bonnie is allergic to cheese. I was, in retrospect rather stupidly, shunning it also to keep her company, so we declined the offer. They looked at us as if we had two heads. Just as Bonnie was telling me to explain our refusal, Lucien, Lulu's formidable husband and *patron de la maison* (owner and boss of the domaine), asked us why we didn't partake of the cheese balls. When I told him of Bonnie's cheese allergies, he said with disdain, "C'est ridicule. Ce n'etait pas un médecin Francais qui vous a dit ca." It's ridiculous. It wasn't (couldn't have been) a French doctor who told you that. Ironically, it was. He went on to tell us that the penicillin in the cheese was "good for us." OK. Not a very auspicious start.

When we sat down to lunch—this was just before Easter—we were then served what must have been a traditional Provençal, or Tempier, Easter lunch. The first course was cold sardines (were they uncooked?) in olive oil. The other guests were sliding them down their throats with relish, the young Americans as well. Bonnie and I acknowledged with a glance, shuddering slightly, that we better get them sliding down our throats too. The texture was not to my liking, but we made it through.

Next course. We weren't quite prepared for a goat stew with the horns and hooves still attached and prominently visible. Am I a squeamish eater? I hadn't thought so, but French dishes like *pied de porc* or *tête de veau* are singularly unappealing to me. I am absolutely not into eel either. Anyway, after our initial shock and trepidation, the meal was delicious, as it was served with pasta in black-truffle sauce. I had more pasta than goat. The American kids? They never blinked and gobbled everything down.

I was really psyched for a meal with Lulu at Domaine Templier. But, I must say, I would have preferred rack of lamb. Regardless, it was obviously a memorable meal, and we were most fortunate to have been included. That's especially so now that both Lulu and Lucien are gone. They were bigger than life. Lulu, too, in spite of being barely five feet tall.

How were the wines, you ask? The reds were powerful and distinctive but, honestly, it's the food that I remember best, and that's a rarity.

An Adventure, Dining and Otherwise, in Vieux Lyon

One year, it may have been in 1990, Bonnie and I decided to go to Vieux Lyon for a mini vacation. Driving south on the Autoroute de Soleil, we went past Lyon, which is always confusing, and I missed my exit. Not a happy occurrence. We had flown into Geneva from Zurich and rented a car that, unbeknownst to me, had Italian plates. I took the next exit and got off the autoroute as soon as I could. There we were, as far as I was concerned, in the middle of nowhere. No GPS or cell phones back then. I saw an older couple, midseventies, walking on the sidewalk, and I stopped to ask them directions back to Vieux Lyon. When they noticed the Italian plates, they started singing some Italian songs. Laughingly, I said, "No, no, we're Americans." So they started singing our National Anthem. They were very sweet and cute. I explained where I wanted to go, and they gave me detailed directions.

All was good, but when I got to a complex point of the road, I was again stymied. There was a briskly moving young woman on the sidewalk, so I stopped and asked her how I could get to Vieux Lyon. I knew it had to be close. She looked at me, then her watch. She then asked me "C'est votre femme?" Is that your wife there with you? I said yes. She said, "Bon, OK. I will show you," and she jumped in the back seat and directed me where to go. I had to go down an alley so narrow I thought we were going to scrape the mirrors off. But we got there. She waved off my thanks and bounced off to wherever she had to go. I still wasn't yet 100 percent out of the woods, even though I could see our hotel in the distance. To protect Vieux Lyons from traffic, they had these iron balls that come up out of the pavement, blocking traffic. I was looking at it stupidly, wondering what to do when all of a sudden, it happily sank back down into the ground, and I could proceed.

Lyon, as many know, is a revered gastronomical area of France, with loads of fabulous restaurants serving elegant yet hearty cuisine distinctive to their region. Vieux Lyon dates back to the fifteenth/sixteenth century and is a protected historic area. Lyon itself is an interesting, bustling city, perhaps more rustic than Paris, but with a subdued power and energy of its own. The section called Vieux Lyon is a neat area to walk around, as it abounds with interesting shops, cafés, and restaurants.

We stayed at a fabulous hotel right in Old Lyon called la Cour de Loge. It had only opened a few years previous to our arrival and was a combo of sleek and elegant mixed with old-world charm. We loved it then and would undoubtedly love it today. They now have a fine restaurant attached, but not back then. At any rate, we had reserved a table at a highly acclaimed Michelin two-starred restaurant, La Tour Rose. They now also operate a hotel because to maintain star status with the Michelin Guide, restaurants are obliged to be full service, whether they want to or not. As if they haven't got enough to do just running the restaurant.

At any rate, we got to the restaurant around eight-thirty, and the place was already almost all filled. As Bonnie has a few food allergies, there were not many viable appetizer options for her. We settled on a *mi-cuit* (half-cooked) salmon dish that was only served for two. I thought that although this was a safe choice for her, it might be a bit bland for me, but I didn't really care. Then I noticed that 50 percent of the tables were ordering this same dish. It was a house specialty and was absolutely delicious, with great texture, flavor, and style. For my main course I ordered *rouget fillets* (red mullet, a traditional southern French dish) served on lentils. This is a relatively hearty dish, so I wanted to order a red wine. Again, this must have been around 1990. I spotted a 1985 Pommard Clos des Epenots from Comte Armand on the list at a reasonable price. I knew it had to be off-the-charts great, even though I had never had that vintage. When I placed my order with my server he said, "Ca, c'est tres puissant, monsieur." That wine, it's very (meaning too) powerful, sir. I said, "I know but I *love* the power." After some air, the wine smoothed out, and its tannins softened further once sampled with dinner. It was big yet silky, with lots of old-vine sap and pinot noir spice, broad shouldered but not inelegant or rustic. It really was married to our food. Young red Burgundies, unlike Bordeaux, which are often cabernet sauvignon or merlot based, can be enjoyed young, as they are thinner skinned and have less tannins than those. And they have that ineffable seductive silkiness that no other wine from anywhere can duplicate.

Obviously, this was a memorable bottle enjoyed during a memorable meal enjoyed on an unforgettable vacation.

Mas de Gourgonnier—Baux en Provence

The usual shape of Mas de Gourgonnier's bottle was what first caught my eye before I ever tasted the wine. If you don't know, Mas de Gourgonnier comes in a squatty bottle that does not lend itself well to fitting on wine racks; display bins yes, wine racks no. When I first sampled it over thirty years ago, I was taken by the quality at the price. However, the bottle gave me cause for concern. At the time, I was with an importer with whom I had been working very closely, and he was as conflicted by it as was I. Eventually, we worked out a price for the wine that made sense for both of us and finally I said, "Sure, why not?" and ordered one hundred cases. It has been a staple of my shop ever since and over the years has been one of the most consistent sellers that either one of us has ever had. This importer most graciously allowed me to import the wine myself directly from the estate when I got my import license in 1989.

Mas de Gourgonnier has been in the Cartier family for several generations. The estate is now in the capable hands of the very nice Luc and Sabine Cartier. Luc's brother, Frédéric, is involved as well and works with Luc to keep things running smoothly. The wine, which is a blend of different grape varieties, is invariably delicious when young, but I have had fifteen- and twenty-year-old bottles at dinner with Luc that were shockingly fresh and youthful. I, personally, would prefer to drink the wine on release, but it is nice to know that if you lose a bottle in your cellar and find it years later it has a great shot at being better than good. The blend varies each year depending on which grape varieties were most successful that vintage, so the percentage of what is included in the blend differs yearly. For example, the 2012 was produced from approximately 38 percent cabernet sauvignon, 33 percent carignan, 20 percent grenache, and 9 percent syrah. The 2014 was 35 percent grenache, 24 percent syrah, 24 percent cabernet sauvignon, and 17 percent carignan. Next year it will change.

It should be mentioned, however, that the blend for the US market is not the same as the one for Europe. First of all, the final blend for the United States will differ from the European version, sometimes significantly, because Peter Vezan, who has represented the estate for over thirty years, is allowed to do the US blend each year. He comes to the estate to taste and, working with Luc, determines which casks will be included that year and, therefore, what will be the final blend for the US market. I have been with Peter on several occasions while he is figuring out the blend, and it is interesting and informative to help and see how the pragmatic decisions are made. The wine for the US market is always bottled unfined and unfiltered.

Most years Mas de Gourgonnier has a bouquet that is evocative of plums, raspberries, and Provençal spice (lavender, thyme, rosemary). On the palate, there are flavors of chocolate, caramel, sandalwood, raspberries, lavender, ginger, cinnamon, and nutmeg. It is always a concentrated wine, full yet soft on the palate, often with silty, fine tannins, and no excess alcohol. As it sells for between fifteen and twenty dollars a bottle, I have always felt it's as good a wine for the price as you could ever hope to find.

If ever you were to visit the area, from the property of Mas de Gourgonnier it would take around twenty minutes to get to the charming, tiny medieval town of Eygalières and about thirty minutes to Les Baux, passing through Saint-Rémy-de-Provence on the way. The property itself is gorgeous and consists of forty-seven hectares of vines (nearly one hundred acres) and twenty hectares of olive trees. It is set off from the beaten path, seemingly in the middle of nowhere, with nothing else around. The clear open air of the domaine is pollution free. Another plus is that there are no bothersome neighbors close by using pesticides that could blow back on their vines, so they are able to grow grapes that are certified organic.

All the products of the *mas* (farm) are certified by ECOCERT (the French certification-control body). Luc uses only biological farming methods, following the "Nature and Progress" laws, which forbid any use of chemical fertilizer, weed killer, or insecticide. Only natural fertilizers are used. The summer weather is usually very hot, dry, and windy, just the perfect climate for growing healthy grapes, and those they only pick by hand. The wine is fermented on natural (wild) yeasts, then aged in a combination of tank and older French oak barrels (*foudre*), then bottled unfined and unfiltered. They do the bottling themselves at the domain. These are all positives for the vine.

Vacationing in Les Baux

Getting back to Eygalières, it is a great place to vacation or just or to visit. Bonnie and I have spent many summers there, usually at a charming, very fairly priced old property called Mas de la Brune. Part of their property features an amazing, extensive horticultural area called Le Jardin de l'Alchimiste, which is far more than a garden, with all kinds of exotic plantings. The gorgeous grounds of Mas de la Brune are encircled with lavender, and there is a neat swimming pool area. In July, the region averages only two days of rain and has no humidity, and I find the ineffable, clear air due to the Alpille location intoxicating. But when the mistral blows, which it may in the late fall, one has to duck for cover.

Saint-Rémy-de-Provence, with its abundance of charm and good restaurants, is less than twenty minutes away from Eygalières, with Les Baux under thirty. However, the Bistro de Eygalières is a small, yet elegant, dynamite restaurant that I highly recommend. Killer rack of lamb and super wines from the region. The Romans spent quite a bit of time in this area, and Roman ruins abound. There is a minuscule medieval city in Eygalières—people actually live there—but the medieval city at Les Baux is far larger and more interesting. At one time four thousand people lived there. Today there are reportedly just twenty-two residents. If you have never been to Les Baux and you are anywhere close, it is a must. The surrounding Alpille Mountains are eerily like a moonscape and are unique and visually captivating.

Les Baux is a tourist magnet in the summer, as it is considered one of the most picturesque villages in France. It has a spectacular position in the Alpilles Mountains, on a rocky outcrop featuring a ruined castle that overlooks the plains to the south. The Celts used the site as a fortification, and traces of habitation were found there that date back as far as 6000 BC.

The best restaurant and hotel in the Les Baux area is L'Oustau de Baumaniere. Bonnie and I had an unbelievably wonderful, beyond-three-star, dinner there once, dining outside under the stars, looking at the incomparable mountains. We had their signature dish, duck for two, served two ways. I had ordered, against the rather gruff sommelier's advice, a bottle of 1995 Châteauneuf du Pape-Château Pignan, from the Château Rayas property. Great meal, great night, great wine, and indelible memories.

Languedoc

The Languedoc encompasses a *huge* area in the middle of the south of France, reportedly 10,570 square miles. It stretches from the Rhône Valley in the east to the Spanish border in the southwest. It is made up of five departments, four of which are Mediterranean coastal departments. They are the Gard, the Hérault, the Aude, and the Eastern Pyrenees or Pyrénées-Orientales. The fifth is the inland department of Lozère, which forms the southern bastion of the Massif Central.

Almost three million people live in the Languedoc. Many of them must be in the wine business, because over a third of the total wine produced in France comes from there. No longer can most of it be regarded merely as "plonk." And we do hope that no dark, pungent, and powerful Languedoc wines are clandestinely added to expensive wines in Bordeaux and Burgundy to add depth, as was reportedly done in the far distant past by some. One would assume that the "wine police" have effectively eliminated this nefarious practice of yesteryear, right?

There are many areas of the Languedoc that offer good wine at fair prices. Here are some of the ones I like the best: Fitou, Saint-Chinian, Faugères, Pic-St-Loup, Corbières, Minervois, Mont-peyroux, Côte de Thongue, and Costières de Nîmes. There are even excellent Champagne-like sparkling wines, Crémant de Limoux, from Aude. Over the years, I have done business in some fashion or another with growers in all of the above-named areas but, unfortunately, many have been dropped from our portfolio for one reason or another.

Anne Gros and Jean-Paul Tollot—Minervois

Anne Gros has gotten the itch, as have other Burgundians before her, to go down south to the Languedoc to buy some prime, not expensive, property and make great, Burgundy-inspired southern French wine. She and her partner, Jean-Paul Tollot, owner of Domaine Tollot-Beaut, found what they were looking for outside the tiny village of Cazelles: fourteen hectares (about thirty acres) located at the high, northern edge of the Minervois appellation. Anne says she knew she had found what she wanted as soon as she saw the property, which has a diverse, stony/mineral terroir. It is located on the Minervois/Saint-Chinian border and, remarkably, is at the same elevation as some of Vosne-Romanee's 1er Crus.

Aside from the venerable old-vines vineyards, which require a tremendous amount of work to sustain and maintain, they are blessed with a climate great for growing grapes. The nights are relatively cool even during the summer heat. Anne, Jean-Paul, and their four kids spend most of their weekends enjoying the area and working in the fields. They have invested a tremendous amount of time, energy, and money on this project and seem to be succeeding. They want to feature local grape varieties such as the not-as-well-known cinsault and carignan, as well as the more accepted syrah and grenache. The wines produced so far have been very well received and are full-bodied, rich, and powerful, yet they all have an underlying sense of elegance and, dare I say, finesse not found in wines from this region. Of course, the love, effort, and money spent on these wines are unparalleled.

The wines are not inexpensive, but, price to quality, they are very strong and would give many higher-priced southern Rhône wines, like Châteauneuf du Pape, a run for their money. The wine press has been on board, and there are quite a few restaurants here and abroad that are serving them—Bar Balud in Boston for one. The question, as it always is with these types of unknown wines, is will the public get on board, can the quality and demand be sustained and increased. And, for Anne and Jean-Paul, can they ever make any money doing this. School's out for now, but Anne is one determined lady. I would never bet against her, regardless of the odds.

Domaine Pierre Clavel

Certainly one of my favorite Languedoc producers, one with whom I have done consistent business for years, is Pierre Clavel; I even sold his father's wine way back when. I always get a chuckle out of Pierre. He is of medium height, sturdily built and strikingly handsome, with an enviable thick mop of white-gray hair on top of a weathered face that features eye crinkles. He has an infectious, pixyish, boyish grin when happy. If you were to Google his image you can clearly see that he likes the way he looks. I find him, bright, personable, sometimes moody, often funny, and very hardworking. Today Pierre's work is aided by his wife, Estelle, and their two sons, Antoine and Martin.

Pierre began making wine in 1986. He now owns thirty-three hectares of appellation Languedoc vineyards outside of Montpelier, not far from the Mediterranean Sea. The vines are planted in rocky soils, similar to those of Châteauneuf du Pape, with heavy stones called *galets* covering large portions of them. His red wines, Le Mas, Les Garrigues, and La Copa Santa, all come from the sloped vineyards at La Méjanelle, where sandstone rocks retain the heat during the day, which is then slowly released during the colder evenings, helping the grapes to ripen evenly. Again, à la Châteauneuf du Pape, the hot and dry Mediterranean climate helps to concentrate the grapes, and the sea breezes mixed with the northern Mistral keep the vines bug and disease free. For the past several years, Clavel's viticulture has been certified 100 percent organic.

One of my favorite wines from Domaine Clavel, along with their terrific, inexpensive rosé, is their least expensive red, Le Mas. In the past, vintages of Le Mas have made *Wine Advocate*'s "World's Greatest

Wine Values" list and have been featured in *Wine Spectator*, but his past several vintages are better than those ever were. Made from a blend of approximately 50 percent syrah/50 percent grenache, the wine has a dark purple color with a lovely bouquet of Provencal herbs and spices (*garrigue*). It is full and soft on the palate, with plenty of punch, an aftertaste of spice and cassis, with fine, well-integrated tannins. You would never guess that it sells for under fifteen dollars a bottle. It offers delicious drinking pleasure with up-front fruit just bursting through. It and other Clavel wines are found on many sophisticated wine lists both in the United States and in France.

Montpellier

Montpellier, the Languedoc-Roussillon's capital city, would be another vacation spot that is off the beaten path, not necessarily first thought of, but fun. It is an interesting city that has wide streets lined with large, shady trees, a large pedestrian-only central square that was laid out in the 1700s, and shopping that is supposed to be good, with chic boutiques and interesting shops. The architecture in the city is different from elsewhere in France and is interesting. Montpellier's pedestrian-only Rue de la Loge goes into the ancient, most attractive part of town known as l'Ecusson. If you were to visit the area in the summer, I am told there is a beach close by, but I have never had the time to go sit.

Of course, for wine lovers, there are many excellent wineries, like Clavel's, that would be delighted to see you and sell you a bottle or two for a picnic.

Domaine de l'Aigueliere and Domaine Peyre Rosé—Coteaux du Languedoc

Domaine de l'Aigueliere, Coteaux du Languedoc, and Domaine Peyre Rosé, Coteaux du Languedoc, are both from the Hérault region, with vineyards not far from the Mediterranean Sea. When I first started working with them, they were two unknown domaines that offered exceptionally concentrated Rhône-style wines at fabulously low prices. Once they gained renown, demand in France increased and the prices rose significantly. They became too expensive for the quality or for them to be competitive in the US market. Even with me working on short margins to try to keep placements, interest dwindled, so we reluctantly had to say goodbye to both. For years I had sold many cases of these wines to savvy buyers, so these were painful losses for me. But if we construe something to be no longer a value, even if still good, we need to take a walk. It's a tough, subjective decision that all customers have to make, not just with wine.

Marlene Soria, of Peyre Rosé, really was someone special, though. Her property was off the grid for years, relying on donkeys for power, if you can imagine that. Tasting with her was a trip. When the electric company finally came to offer to tie her in, she refused. "I managed all these years without you. I see no reason to change now." Wow! Talk about independent women.

Vouvray

Domaine Georges Brunet

Like Pouilly-Fuissé, there are as many different styles and qualities of Vouvray as there are growers. Most, again like Pouilly-Fuissé, make facile wine that goes down easily but doesn't necessarily excite. But there are growers in both of these areas of France who care enough to transform hard work and excellent vineyard sites into memorable wine. Wines from those growers have that ineffable French *gout de terroir*, the taste of the vineyard site, and have soul. Daniel Barraud and Jean Pierre Auvigue work that way in Pouilly-Fuissé, and Nicolas Brunet of Domaine Georges Brunet works that way in Vouvray.

In March 2014 I visited the Vouvray domaine of Georges Brunet with my retail general manger, Alex Bluhm. It has been run for some time by the very hardworking, very personable Nicolas Brunet. Nicolas, who appears to be in his midthirties, is tall and slim, with long, brown, wavy hair and dark, prominent eyebrows. He is a highly intelligent man who is passionate about his craft. Nicolas also has a keen sense of humor and an infectious joie de vivre. He spent a long time with us tasting in his amazing limestone caves, dug out by hand. He showed us how he has kept enlarging the caves by digging them out himself with a pick and shovel, tunneling through, if you will. Also memorable was the small, deep, low, and unlit cave where his family cached and hid some of their wine treasures from the ever-rapacious Nazis. I was happy to have a pocket flashlight with me, and this was another occasion that I was glad not to be six feet tall.

Vouvray is another wine that is made 100 percent from one grape variety, like Bourgogne Rouge is made 100 percent from pinot noir or Barolo 100 percent from nebbiolo. In the case of Vouvray, the grape variety is chenin blanc. When Nicolas first showed us the wines he wanted us to try, we were initially skeptical. His offer to taste his 2007 and 2008 Vouvrays did not inspire us with confidence, as older-vintage whites, even from Vouvray, usually are faded or worse. But after tasting these wines we were quickly won over. They showed more freshness and were more youthful than some 2012s from other less conscientious producers. These Vouvrays were clear, mineral tinged, and lively, bursting with tart, green-apple fruit. Both vintages were balanced by a lively, bright, fresh acidity and they aged exceedingly well. Their added complexity comes from the vineyard's terroir of limestone, flint, and minerals.

The Vouvray Sec was, naturally, the drier of the two, but not by much. There was a beautiful pear/tangerine flavor that was anything but cloying in the demi-sec, as it had a perfectly balanced, trailing acidity. It was being served by the glass in one of my favorite local restaurants, the excellent Il Capriccio Ristorante located in Waltham, Massachusetts. Owner Richie Baron was serving grilled chicken livers with grilled onions in a sauce of balsamic vinaigrette. I thought the combination of the balsamic reduction with the crisp, semisweet 2007 Demi-Sec Vouvray from Brunet, with its dry finish, would work out just fine. It was better than that. The crisp acidity and the natural noncloying sweetness of the wine married that dish, and it was as good as or better than anything one could find at a five-star restaurant. The dish was thirteen dollars, and so was the glass of wine. Who says you have to pay megabucks for a quality culinary experience?

We were also very impressed with the very favorable price points for the quality. We were definitely buyers but, ultimately, we couldn't decide whether to buy the 2008 Vouvray sec or the 2007 Vouvray demi-sec, so we ended up buying both. They were both still very youthful and showed the rarely seen classic style of chenin blanc found in bottle-aged Vouvrays. Only the best Vouvrays are capable of aging and improving, and they are few. I, frankly, don't how Brunet does it for the price, except they do own the land.

While exploring the cave, we noticed a pile of dusty magnums (1.5L bottles) of Demi-Sec Vouvray dating from 1995. We asked, "These bottles are still labeled; how is that possible?" Most bottles this old would have labels that would either be peeling off or, more likely, would have been long gone. These looked to be perfectly intact.

Nicolas smiled and pulled out a bottle to show us. He explained that for this special vintage they had etched their label into the glass, so there was nothing to peel off. The bottles were really beautiful, very attractive. He then surprised us by asking if we would like him to open one. We looked at each other somewhat startled and said, "Absolutely, let's do it!"

Our initial assumption was that these bottles were still in the cellar only as examples to demonstrate to visiting wine professionals the ageability of his wines. While they certainly had that, we soon were shocked and amazed by the freshness and quality of the wine. The bouquet in the 1995 Brunet Vouvray Demi-Sec was stunning, ethereal, and unforgettable. It opened up instantly, with an aroma redolent of honeysuckle and honeyed fruits. A lush palate of stone fruit, melon, and spicy clove complemented the nose gracefully. At a very modest twenty grams of residual sugar per liter, the clean, bright acidity balanced this wine to perfection. It was the mouth feel that really knocked us out. The silky texture, the balanced complexity, the tight structure gave us the immediate desire to have some more! This was much too good to spit out. Careful; we hadn't eaten yet. What really rocked our world was when Nicolas asked if we would like a couple of cases to offer for sale in Massachusetts. We jumped at the chance and ended up buying, and selling, five six-bottle cases, one bottle maximum, to thirty happy people, most of whom served them on Thanksgiving that year. Would that all my visits were so informative, fun, and beneficial; alas, they are not.

After the extensive tasting, Nicolas finally took us out to his various vineyards. It was late afternoon by this time, and I was tired and getting hungry. Do I really need to see another vineyard? However, it was worth the time and trouble. Nicolas, who speaks excellent English, was justly proud of his vineyard work. His years of sustainable and natural vineyard-management techniques have paid off. Unfortunately, he cannot get certification for organic grapes because his vines are in such close proximity to those of his neighbors, plural, who do not follow his organic approach. Regardless, he has been working his vineyards organically for years and continues to do so. The clearly seen differences between Nicolas's vineyards and those of his neighbors were startling. His rows of vines were straight, clean, and healthy. His neighbor's vineyards looked sickly by comparison. He is also one of only four growers in Vouvray to still hand harvest, out of 160 currently producing in the appellation. There is a reason his wines are so good.

It is important to note that the Brunet family has been producing wine in the village of Vouvray for eight generations. This is not a new enterprise. Their fourteen hectares of vineyard are on clay, limestone, and flinty soils. They have three cellars cut into the limestone hillsides where they vinify. Again, all harvesting is done by hand, and they only use stainless steel, to preserve the freshness of the fruit.

Bordeaux

Bankrupt in Bordeaux?

It is often said, "If you want to make a little money in the wine business, start with big money." For certain driven multimillionaire vineyard owners in California this is no surprise, nor is it a detriment. These people may have the resources and patience to sustain losses and not feel excessive pain because they *love* the business, and they can "write it off." It *was* a surprise for certain Bordeaux château owners who are in serious financial trouble, with many of them on the verge of bankruptcy. How is that possible? Bordeaux is a vast appellation, with 190,000 acres of vineyards and over 10,000 wine properties, most of which are small, comprising less than twenty acres. Only 5 percent of the "great estates" belong to the prestigious Union des Grands Crus, and only a fraction of them are from the Classified Château, which are so sought after worldwide.

Jean-Guillaum Pratts, managing director of Châteaux, Cos d'Estournel, says, "There are two Bordeaux. We (the top châteaux owners) have sold our wines at outrageous prices while right next door there were people who were not surviving." One case of Cos today sells for more than one hundred cases of generic Bordeaux. Paradoxically, while prices for classified Bordeaux have never been higher, prices for the lesser lights of Bordeaux are so low that many cannot survive. Many young growers who went deeply into debt to buy their vineyards are on the verge of losing everything—homes included.

Much of the responsibility for this situation must rest with the Bordelaise themselves. For the past twenty years untold acres of agricultural land in Bordeaux unsuitable for viticulture were turned into vineyards anyway. The large quantity of wine produced may not have been particularly good, but the demand was there, and greed prevailed. Of course there had to be a loud wake-up call. Ultimately, inventories backed up as people got wise, and there was a glut on the market.

Global competition is fierce, with many people interested in drinking quality, not quantity. Even the French themselves are drinking far less (but better) than they used to, especially in Provençal restaurants, where the cops wait to alcohol test patrons before they drive off. So, hundreds of châteaux owners are in desperate financial trouble, including some quality-oriented petit châteaux that have unfairly been tarred with the same brush.

Things will ultimately improve for the truly quality-oriented châteaux, if they can hang in. The others? They might consider the offer by the French government of a subsidy to convert their vineyards to commercially viable, high-demand crops, such as corn, rapeseed, or sunflowers. With the ever-increasing demand for biofuel, oil seeds are in huge demand. So as distasteful as it may be for the grape grower/vigneron to uproot his vines, he could convert, keep his farm, and make a good living growing oil seeds with the aid and blessing of the government. No more headaches trying to find vineyard workers: you just sow, reap, and cash in! Those reluctant to do so will undoubtedly get a firm nudge, or kick in the backside, from their banker.

Château Prieuré-Lichine with Alexis Lichine

On my first buying trip to France I was traveling with the owner of a small import/distribution company with whom I was friendly and whose palate and wine selections I respected. We first went to Burgundy, where he showed me the then graphic differences between *négociant* wine and wine produced by smaller, hands-on growers. Today, firms like Jadot, Drouhin, Bichot, Faiveley et al. produce wines as *négociants* in the same manner as the independent growers and offer wines that most often rival the quality of their smaller counterparts. Back in the early '80s the difference was marked.

I was particularly excited to go on this trip, as I had just started studying French six months prior to departure and wanted to know how I would manage with the language once in France. I was gratified to at least be able to understand some of the words and get the gist of most of the conversations, but I could only speak a pidgin French that was barely comprehensible. But I was very much encouraged. I had thought that after six months of study I would be speaking fluent French. Lots of luck with that. Two to five years would be more realistic if one didn't live in the country for a while. As I have written previously, learning French at forty years of age without ever spending any time living in France was one of the hardest things I have ever done, and one of the things of which I am the most proud.

After spending a few days in Burgundy, we headed for Bordeaux, where we stayed two nights at Château Prieuré-Lichine. Of course, I knew that Prieuré-Lichine was a Margaux classified as a Fourth Growth, based on Bordeaux's 1855 classification. But I knew nothing about the owner, Alexis Lichine. Alexis, as it turns out, had had an interesting life. At the time that I met him he was sixty-seven years old. Alexis was born in Moscow in 1913, but he and his family escaped to France during the Russian Revolution of 1917. They left France for the United States in 1919. Alexis went to the University of Pennsylvania, where he studied economics, but he never stayed long enough to get a degree. He tried and failed as a wine importer, worked retail at a shop in New York, and finally, after receiving his American citizenship, was hired by estimable wine merchant, Frank Schoonmaker, as his national sales manager.

During World War II, he served in the US Army Military Intelligence in Europe and North Africa and was discharged as a major. After the war, Alexis asked Frank Schoonmaker for full partnership in the company. Frank said no, and Alexis left to work for the import wine division of United Distillers of America. In 1950, after bouncing around, working at a number of wine-related jobs, he became the export manager for Château Haut-Brion. In 1951 he bought Château Prieuré-Lichine and in 1952 became part owner and manager of Château Lascombes. In '55, living in Margaux, he founded Alexis

Lichine Négociants and Lichine & Cie and finally became a successful exporter of fine wines.

I knew very little of this at the time. I was just excited to be in Bordeaux at a famous château. I had no need to speak French with Alexis, but I soon found that my English wasn't necessarily sufficient either. We met Alexis late afternoon. He was very tall, well over six feet, quite formidable looking, with a rather stern, unsmiling visage, lots of graying hair, and great, bushy eyebrows. He was a bit gruff. I am sure he had lots of things he would have preferred doing than having another tasting late in the day. Of course, since he wasn't young and had considerable bulk, maybe his feet hurt? Anyway, we tasted through some bottled wines and a few cask samples.

Finally, I gathered my courage to ask him a question. Up until then I was merely an almost invisible observer and listener. Proud of my use of a French word I asked, "So, Alexis, what is the *encépagement* (grape varieties included) for Prieuré-Lichine?" He continued on as if he had heard nothing. Hmm. I tried again, "What is the *encépage* of Prieuré-Lichine?" He talked for a few moments about other things then, finally, he turned and looked at me directly and said, "Look, I can tell you the percentage of grapes that we plant at the château, but that doesn't mean I can accurately tell you the percentage of those grapes that are included in the final bottling. Look over there," he said, "through that window. You see all those stacked-up wooden cases marked Château Clairfont? Clairfont is the second label of Prieuré-Lichine. At *assemblage* (when the final casks are chosen to be included in the Grands Châteaux) we taste through all the casks and only then decide which ones will make up Prieuré-Lichine and which ones will be declassed to Château Clairfont. Each year is different. Some years the merlot is more successful than the cabernet, so there is a higher percentage of merlot in Prieuré that year. Other years it's the reverse. We never know the exact *encépagement* of Prieuré in any given year, just the percentage of grapes we grow at the château." Oh, OK. This I could understand, and it made perfect sense.

The same is true of all châteaux that have second-label wines. Château Pichon Lalande has Reserve de la Comtese. Château Leoville

Las Cases has Clos du Marquis etc. The second-label wines from Grands Châteaux offer excellent value, as they are wines produced from casks that for whatever reason were not accepted to be included in the final blend but *are* of the château. They may not live as long or be as complex, but they will show the pedigree and cost far less.

Alexis Lichine died of cancer at Château Prieuré-Lichine on June 1, 1989, at seventy-six years of age. His son Sacha, who I knew slightly when he worked briefly at the now defunct C. Pappas Co. in Boston, sold Prieuré-Lichine in August of 1999. In 2008, Alexis Lichine was posthumously inducted into the Wine Writers' Hall of Fame by the Wine Media Guild of New York. I have a copy of his book *The Wines of France*, copyright 1955, in my office today. I will always remember meeting him.

Bordeaux as Futures; Should We Buy?

Should we buy Bordeaux as futures? That is always a subjective decision that depends on a number of variables. Between March and June, I traditionally begin receiving quotes on Bordeaux as futures. Not long ago, Bordeaux futures were either sought after frenetically in acclaimed, very good to great vintages or were completely ignored. I believe that the lack of interest for the 2011, 2012, and 2013 vintages had less to do with lukewarm reviews than the fact that most of us are fed up with brokers of classified châteaux arrogantly assuming that wine enthusiasts can't live without their latest vintage. They expect us to queue up annually, cash in hand, regardless of the price or quality, to vie for wine that won't be seen for two years and won't be ready to enjoy for at least another five.

In the distant past, a merchant in a good year could afford to buy Classified Growths from Bordeaux as futures, sell 50 percent or so in advance, and then own the rest at prices that were well below the market when the wines did arrive one to two years later. That doesn't happen today.

Merchants may offer some Bordeaux as futures, always at substantially reduced markups, but very few have the resources to stock up. The same is true of hotels and fine restaurants that used to do so regularly. With Bordeaux futures prices currently so high, even at the initial offering, *à la première tranche*, prices are just as likely to stay the same, or drop, as to go up. And very few, especially Americans, get the low, initial offering prices. You think the stock market is risky?

I started out in the wine business as a Bordeaux specialist fifty-plus years ago. I have pretty much seen it all. What amazes me is how many Bordeaux power brokers continue to be so insular. Apparently, for them knowledge is not cumulative; they seem to never learn from past mistakes. Part of the problem for Bordeaux is due to the wine media overextolling the virtues of the very best vintages as well as emphasizing the negatives of those less good; however, many of the wounds from which the Bordelais suffer are self-inflicted. Most are so far removed from reality that prices are arbitrarily set not based on quality, or even quantity, but on what they think they can get— regardless of currency fluctuations.

Why would they have raised prices on a mediocre, albeit pleasant, year like 1997, charging more for them than for the far better 1996s? It doesn't compute. In years like 1995, 2000, 2005, and 2009 they could more or less write their own ticket, as initial demand was so high. The supply for those could never satisfy the worldwide demand of all those interested in buying Classified Growths. But why charge excessively for years like 1997, 1998, 1999 not to mention the really poor years of 1991, 1992, 1993, and 1994? Wouldn't it have made better economic sense to have initially priced the wines from the nongreat years lower than previous good vintages, rather than higher? Hello. Wouldn't the wine media have regarded these years more sympathetically if the prices were at least "fair" or reasonable? If they had been priced correctly from go, might they not have sold through more quickly and not have to be dumped at a loss at a later date?

Prices on the 2009s were the highest we had ever seen, only to be eclipsed by the 2010s. Both vintages, admittedly, are of extremely high quality. That's fine, but for the less good 2011 vintage as futures there was only a 20 percent drop in price? A 20 percent drop meant that the 2011 futures were actually priced higher than the 2009s first offerings. This makes sense? Unfortunately, while certain estates like Leoville Barton always price very fairly at the beginning of a futures campaign, many other Classified Growths try to extract as much as they think they can get.

The Bordeaux from the 2011, 2012, and 2013 vintages were not exceptional, First Growths not withstanding. Are there some good wines, especially some easy-drinking 2012s? Sure, but should they even be considered as futures? There were horrible weather conditions for those years, so there is a good reason why quality suffered. However, it was universally understood that 2011 would be among the most difficult vintages in years for them to sell as futures, unless prices were to drop substantially. They didn't drop nearly enough, ditto 2012. So, once again they sit with too much unwanted, unloved wine.

If everyone who was even cursorily interested knew this would occur, why couldn't the power moguls in Bordeaux see it too? Let's remember, I am referring specifically to châteaux included in the 1855 classification: First Growths like Lafite, Margaux, Mouton, Latour, and Haut Brion, down to Fifth Growths like Lynch Bages, Grand Puy Lacoste, and Pontet Canet. Huge egos are involved, and I guess that trumps good business sense.

The 2011 vintage may actually have radically affected how business is done in Bordeaux for years to come, and it could end futures campaigns forever. In fact, the owners of Château Latour have stopped futures sales on their wines for this year. Owners of other classifieds are furious. But Latour is ahead of the game and thinking correctly. Of course, they have the resources to hunker down and wait to offer their wine when they deem it ready. It will be interesting to see what ultimately transpires.

The irony is that there are, in fact, increasingly available amounts of Bordeaux, some from châteaux previously unfamiliar to nearly all of us, that offer excellent quality at reasonable prices. Those are the wines Bordeaux lovers should seek out. Ch. Lanessan, Ch. Bernadotte, Ch. d'Escurac, Ch. Lyonat, Ch. le Conseiller, Ch. Croix Mouton,

Ch. Charmail, Ch. Cambon la Pelouse, and many others like them are good, solid wines for the value-conscious consumers who don't have the resources, or feel the need, to chase after the Second and Third Growths now asking hundreds of dollars for their wine.

The reality is that worldwide demand and subsequent pricing of great vintages will probably mean that most Bordeaux lovers will have to trade down and buy some Côtes de Castillon, Bordeaux Sup., Lussac or Puisseguin-Saint Émilion, Côtes du Bourg, Côtes de Fronsac, and/or second labels of the Grand Châteaux to at least augment their purchases. No one will suffer for that. There is a sea of good to very good wine out there, and values do exist.

Tasting in Cask

When I started going on wine-buying trips to France in the '80s, I would often go to Bordeaux. It was important to taste cask samples of the new vintage from various châteaux, as the wines usually aren't bottled for two years. It sounds romantic, but it's not. Rarely would we go to the actual châteaux to taste. When we did go, it was usually disappointing because, as beautiful as they may be, nearly all the classified châteaux are shells, not homes, with many owned by conglomerates such as insurance agencies, etc. Today, fifty or so are now Asian owned, with the Chinese snapping them up at a worrisome rate. They don't live there either.

Our tastings were mainly conducted from cask samples in the offices of *negotiants* in downtown Bordeaux. Cask samples are little four-ounce sample bottles of wine taken directly from the barrel (cask). We, of course, never knew from which cask they were taken, and that makes a difference; casks are not all the same. Some barrels come from the best plots on the vineyard, others from plots that are either less well placed or that have younger vines. And we usually didn't know how long it had been since the sample had been pulled or how it was stored. Samples more than two days old were not helpful, as no preservatives are used and they have a short shelf life.

After trying a dozen or more samples, I inevitably felt in need of a tongue scraper to eliminate the tannins. A beer probably would have worked, but we never experimented or had the chance, which is too bad. With all that tannin coating your tongue, everything pretty much tastes the same. Undoubtedly, Robert Parker and other influential wine writers have access to the actual casks at some of the châteaux when they taste, but not always and not all of them. One does wonder how the casks from which they taste are chosen. The fact is, people around the world, not just in the US, have relied on Parker and others for assessments of the new vintage if they are considering buying Bordeaux as futures. If a wine a gets a 90-point rating, it will sell. The converse is true.

Futures from anywhere should only be bought if all or at least most of the following are true:

1) The wine is from a very good to great vintage.

2) The wine would be difficult or nearly impossible to get when released.

3) The price is certain to go up substantially when the wine arrives, if you could get it at all.

4) Buy only what you have pragmatically researched, wines that you may have had in the past and liked and that you feel comfortable buying. Leave speculating to speculators, who are just as apt to lose as to win. There are no guarantees here. Prices could go up significantly, stay the same, or plummet. You pay your money and you take your chances.

One Can Dine Well in Bordeaux, However

Back in the '80s two colleagues and I went to a restaurant in Bordeaux that was recommended highly to us called Christian … something. I forget the name but know it was the chef's name. Unfortunately, it has now been out of business for years but was a hot bistro back then. The food was OK, not memorable, and the wine we ordered, two different obscure Saint Émilions, was not special either. What was memorable was what happened after dinner. We were given the dessert menu and a *menu de digestifs*, or after-dinner drinks. One of my friends spotted a bottle of 1955 Ch. d'Yquem on the list for what he felt was a ridiculously low price. Saying, "This one's on me," he ordered it.

Let's be clear, I have never ordered Ch. d'Yquem in a restaurant, nor do I ever get a chance to drink it. I have sold many vintages, yes; bought any personally, no. I know how great Ch. d'Yquem is but have never been able to rationalize buying any for myself. That said, the '55 was one of most amazing wines I have ever had, or expect to ever have. First, it was a brilliant, gorgeous burnished copper/gold in color. On the palate, the wine was as brilliant as the color, beautifully balanced between fruit and just the right touch of crisp acidity. The wine was deep, full, and heady, wonderfully long, with complex, still youthful flavors of fresh apricots, honeyed nuts, allspice, an ever-so-long aftertaste, and more. It was like a youthful monk or sage professor who was just crammed to the brim with knowledge yet was down-to-earth, noncondescending, and fun loving despite the erudition. A Bill Gates of a wine. It just had so much to offer. Really, description cannot do it justice. Let me just say that it was one of the greatest, most memorable wines I have ever had.

Here's Jancis Robinson's description of the '55 d'Yquem, twenty-five years *after* we had it: "First wave of picking … with a good yield and very high sugar level. Very classic. 17 Sep to 28 Oct. thirty-three days of picking over forty-two days. Very dark copper. Rich almonds on the nose and with enormous richness, and real life. Very long and gorgeous. Real *gras* (fat) and very long. Round and voluptuous. Drink 1975–2025. Rating: 19/20. (2/2008)"

We had been enjoying the d'Yquem for some time, and it was getting late. I turned to my friend who had magnanimously bought the wine and said, "Why not invite the chef over to share a glass with us?" This was our third bottle of the evening. Although we didn't quite finish the other two, that was still a lot of wine. At first he just glared at me, protectively cupping the bottle, then he relented. "Yeah, sure," he said. "Call him over." The chef was thrilled. We couldn't get rid of him. He stayed with us, nonstop talking for so long that his wife, who was furious, couldn't get him in the kitchen to clean up. I guess we should have offered her a glass too.

Game Dinner at Hotel de France— Gascony, France

Gascony, probably best known as the land of d'Artagnan, Alexander Dumas's famous swashbuckling character in *The Three Musketeers*. It is located in the southwest of France, not too far from Bordeaux. It remains a kind of unspoiled, wild, open area that is off the beaten path. Would I recommend it as a vacation destination? I have only been there twice, and that was just overnight, but it might be worth checking out. I am told that enlightened tourists, many of them French, flock there in the summer and early fall. There are interesting medieval towns and villages, locally called *bastides*, nestled in green rolling hills. The landscape is beautiful, and on a clear day there are distant glimpses of the Pyrenees mountain range. They have a nice climate with lovely, sunny weather. Of course, Gascony is noted for its food, too, especially foie gras and Armagnac.

On one of our buying trips to Bordeaux we decided to detour to Gascony to sample the cuisine at the then highly regarded and still renowned Restaurant de l'Hotel de France. At the time it was noted especially for their *menu de gibier*, or wild game. They offered varieties of venison, quail, duck, really almost anything that could be hunted successfully and cooked. I recall that despite its Michelin stars, it was a rather rustic restaurant. That was really no surprise, considering where it was located. Of course, we all ordered the *menu de gibier*, me with some trepidation. The dinner turned out to be great, however; but that is not what was most memorable.

They had a fabulous wine list with some startlingly reasonable prices. What got the attention of the three of us immediately was the listing for a bottle of 1972 La Tâche-Domaine de la Romanée Conte. We called over the very young sommelier to ask him about this wine. The 1972 was not initially regarded as a particularly good Burgundy vintage, although many did ultimately surprise positively after some aging. This was in the mid-1980s, and one could easily assume that this wine, in this vintage, would be too old. Even with three rabid wine professionals quizzing him, this young sommelier was nonplussed. He just smiled confidently and said, "Wait until you try this wine. It's guaranteed." OK, bring it on.

I have often written that with Burgundies it is far more important to know the vineyard site and the grower rather than the vintage year. Sure, great wines cannot be made without great grapes, and in good to great vintages it is easier for the growers to succeed. However, it's a given that even in great vintage years someone, for whatever reason, will blow the vintage. It is also a given that in less good vintage years, years of the vigneron, the great growers will transcend the vintage and make great wine. This is especially true when dealing with 1er Cru and Grands Crus wines. The reason they have Cru status in the first place is due to the vineyard placement. The 1er Crus are generally found midslope, with excellent sun exposure, and the Grands Crus have even better exposition than that. The villages wines, Hautes Côtes and Bourgogne Rouges, are less well situated and may handle the growing season and bad weather less well, with less healthy grapes.

Back to our bottle of La Tâche. The almost but not quite arrogant sommelier brought the bottle and issued us glassware that I hate: shallow and flat, not what I would ever use for serving Burgundy, and certainly not an older wine. Moment of truth. He poured some for each of us to try. The wine was as pale a pinot noir as I had ever seen, almost translucent. I've had rosés with deeper color. Then I tried the wine. As light as it was, it was firmly structured, as if invisible spiderwebs of thin tensile steel threads were holding it together. It may have been light in body, but it just filled my mouth with exquisite, ethereal, ineffable flavors. Subtle, but distinct, flavors of dried flowers, warm earth, hints of cinnamon spice and other dark fruits and herbs. It was a magical blend of silky lightness and subtle power. This was a very precise, focused wine with its own inimitable style and personality. Just beautiful! Please don't consider this sexist, but it reminded me of a beautiful woman of indeterminate age who may be considered soft at first glance but who actually has an iron will guided by high intellect.

I have been to tastings of DRC wines, and I even visited there once, but rarely have I ever drunk any. This wine from a not-great vintage still captivates my mind.

Italy

Italian Wine Adventures

Vinitaly/Verona

When I started Arborway Imports twenty-five years ago, I began by buying southern French wines but soon segued into other areas of France. It wasn't until I was well into year two of Arborway's existence, however, that I felt secure enough to branch out by importing Italian wines.

I had met Marc de Grazia at a trade tasting and was impressed with him and his portfolio. It was a who's who of Italian producers. I called Marc and asked if he had wine available for me. He said, "Of course. Just come to Vinitaly this year. We'll show you around and introduce you to suitable producers. Also, after the wine fair, we are touring Tuscany and the Piedmont, visiting some of our growers. Why don't you come along?" I did make plans to go to Vinitaly but, stupidly, as I didn't want to commit myself and feel obligated, I said no to the invitation to tour Tuscany and Piedmont. A serious mistake.

So what is Vinitaly? The biggest wine/trade show in the world, over one million square feet of exhibition space. It is held annually in Verona in late March/early April in a huge complex of sixteen or so buildings, each as large as Boston's World Trade Center. You can find the best and the worst of Italian wines there, plus wine from other countries. There are over four thousand exhibitors. (Read more at www.vinitalytour.com.)

When I first arrived, I walked around in a kind of daze, not knowing where to start or how to get around if I did. I finally sorted it out but resolved to learn Italian, which, after some time, I did. When I finally found my way to the impressively large De Grazia tasting area, I was met by Marc and got to work. I was shocked at the quality of the wines available for me: Azelia, Giovanni Manzone, Giovanni Corino, Matteo Correggia, and Moccagatta all from the Piedmont; Uccelliera, Le Cinciole, and others from Tuscany. They were great wines then, and they still are now.

Marc and Iano de Grazia are half-brothers who, respectively, are the founder and managing director of Marc De Grazia Selections. They look nothing alike. Marc, who was brought up in the San Francisco area, started the business in 1980. I'm not sure how he transitioned to Italy, or when, but his Italian is indistinguishable from native speakers, and he also speaks fluent French. He speaks English just like any of us, often spicing his comments with as much good old Anglo Saxon English as Terry Francona. We were simpatico from go. Iano, who must be in his fifties, is six feet tall, heavyset but not fat, very pragmatic and intelligent, relatively calm in his demeanor, but suffers fools badly. He is warm and personable, unless you fall out of his good graces, and is just a great guy to be with.

Marco is shorter, maybe five feet nine, stocky, and solid. His most striking features are his eyes, which are snapping black and penetrating, loaded with obvious intelligence and good humor. And then there's his good-sized, but not out-of-proportion, Roman nose.

His temperament is anything but calm. Charismatic, mercurial, tempestuous, brimming over with energy, he suffers fools even less well than Iano. I've seen him at Vinitaly verbally destroy (it almost came to blows) a wise-guy, know-it-all Italian journalist. And I've seen him at the wine fair, with eyes flashing, banish from his booth growers who had transgressed against previously agreed-upon rules. Marco expresses himself beautifully, clearly, and succinctly in at least three languages. I once asked him to expound on the differences between various cru Baroli. I only wish I had recorded what he said. After going to Vinitaly for the first time and learning how good the De Grazia portfolio was, I kicked my self-righteous self for not going on the tour Marc had invited me on. So when he asked me to go on a similar one the following year, I jumped at the chance. When we set out, Marc was the driver. I sat shotgun.

Our party included an Austrian importer, Christian Lerner, a Japanese importer I knew only as Madame Goda, and a Japanese journalist who was traveling with Madame Goda. Christian was a handsome, very friendly, and bright guy who was fun to be with. The journalist, who was very slight, quiet, and polite, spoke only Japanese. Madame Goda, who was in her late thirties/early forties, spoke only Japanese, or broken English "wine talk." I found her highly amusing even though we didn't communicate directly. The trip from Japan to Italy must have been a killer because, except for when we were in the cellars tasting, this lady crashed. If we were dining, her head was on the table. In the car, she slept. Only when we were tasting did she resuscitate herself. She then asked hard-to-understand questions in English that made no sense even if you could have understood them.

We covered a lot of ground, starting in the Piedmont, where the first night I dined with the so-called Barolo Boys: Elio Altare, Dominico Clerico, Paolo Scavino, Luigi Scavino, Renato Corino, Marco Marengo, and others. The food on this trip was beyond belief or expectation. I remember having some kind of beef carpaccio with the Barolo Boys. At first I was leery to try it, but they convinced me to give it a shot and it was delicious.

The problem was, each day we had fabulous three-hour lunches and four-hour dinners, all in people's homes, and they were home-cooked meals that you couldn't have bought in a restaurant for any amount of money. After the third day, my stomach revolted and just shut down. I remember making it to the Piazzano Estate in Tuscany when I was just starting to recover, but not fully. I had to be careful. We were there for lunch and they were grilling, on a spit, some kind of meat that was held together with twine. It smelled and tasted so good, but I dared only nibble at it.

Marc made no concessions to us, his guests, which was his right, as he was the one paying. We could have stayed home. He loves to talk and hold court with his friends, and that often lasted until very late at night. I wasn't as jet-lagged as the poor Japanese lady, but that didn't mean I wasn't tired. I remember one night she was completely zonked and the rest of us were crashing and looked it as we sprawled out in the living room, just listening to Marc expound in Italian. I had started learning Italian the year before, so I had some rudimentary proficiency, but still I only got a word here or there. The lady of the house, a lovely young woman a bit younger than Marco, took pity on us and said, "Marco, sono stanchi, sono stanchi." Marco, they're tired. A huge understatement. Marc didn't care; he kept on waving his hands and talking. We survived to do it all again the next day.

Once we almost didn't survive. Marco at the wheel, me again shotgun. We were approaching the entrance to the *autostrada* (super-highway). When Marco realized he was heading in the wrong direction, he swerved into the correct lane, cutting off and almost taking out a large Bimmer. I turned to look back, and there was the Bimmer's driver making violent hand signals at us. I have never seen, before or since, such a sequence of obscene hand gestures. And, with a red face, I actually knew what they all meant. Never underestimate the ability of Italians to communicate nonverbally.

Unfortunately, I have never had the opportunity to go on another Italian wine tour with Marco. But I am glad I went on this one.

Mysterious? Nebbiolo—Barolo, Barbaresco, Gattinara

Although Barolo, Barbaresco, and Gattinara, from northern Italy's Piedmont region, have for the past several years produced some of greatest wines in the world, it wasn't always so. In the distant past, Piedmont wines were neither as good as they are today nor as sought after. As the younger generation winemakers, many of whom attended oenological schools, started to take over from "dad," they revolutionized how the wines were made. The old-timers went for quantity over quality. They didn't understand that by green harvesting, cutting back the crop, they would increase the power to the existing grapes and make far better wine that would sell for much more money. Most were distrustful of "modern" methods, to their detriment.

One of the nicest of the Barolo Boys, Elio Altare, a lovely, funny, very bright man, tried to convince his father that the "new" methods that he learned in school would increase, not decrease, profits in spite of lower yields. His dad thought Elio was crazy, as he believed it was against the will of God to not accept nature's bounty as is.

In 1983, Elio started to age wine in casks and soon after got rid of his dad's traditional old *botte*. When his dad saw this, the old man freaked out. He went directly to his lawyer and disinherited Elio and willed the entire estate to Elio's sister, who couldn't have cared less about wine or farming. Talk about uncomfortable situations: Elio, his wife, and their two daughters continued living under the dad's roof until his passing. They simply could not afford to move out. Reportedly, he and his dad never spoke to one another again. It took Elio years to buy back the estate after he passed.

For me, price to quality, Barolo, Barbaresco, and Gattinara offer some of the best values in the world for great wine. But you've got to love and understand them first. Unfortunately, there are even more misconceptions about the great Piedmont reds than there are for red Burgundies, with fewer explanations. While red Burgundies may be mysterious to some wine lovers, Piedmont wines such as Barolo, Barbaresco, and Gattinara may be even more so.

Many people believe that Baroli and other nebbiolo-based wines are similar to Rhône wines, where in fact they far more closely resemble Burgundies. Like red Burgundies, which are made solely from one grape variety, pinot noir, Barolo, Barbaresco, and Gattinara are made *only* from nebbiolo grapes. Nebbiolo is about fruit in much the same way that pinot noir is about fruit. Although there is conjecture as to the origins of the nebbiolo grape, it has many more pinot noir characteristics than syrah/grenache characteristics. Like red Burgundies, they can be less saturated in color than are Rhône wines because nebbiolo grapes, like pinot noir grapes, are thin skinned. But, even when lighter in color, they can show ample, powerful, velvety tannins, with a structured underpinning and a solid fruit/acid balance. They go best with fine foods and, like red Burgundies, have finesse, complexity, and a rapierlike intensity. Again, as with Burgundies, quantities are minuscule, as the Piedmont's properties are microscopic, with an average vineyard size of less than two acres.

Rhône wines tend to be fuller-bodied, deeply fruited, warm, powerful, extroverted wines that go full throttle. Nebbiolo-based wines are more subtle, complex, and elegant, often with flavors of truffles, violets, tar, faded roses, incense, plums, and raspberries. They have gorgeous aromas of rose petals and eucalyptus, dried fruit, herbs, tar, and licorice. With a unique combination of strength and delicacy, fruit and earth, complexity and austerity, these great nebbiolo-based wines are unique and very special in the wine world.

There are considerable, discernible differences between the wines from various villages and vineyards in Barolo, Barbaresco, and Gattinara, much like those found in wines from different Burgundy villages. Tasted side by side, wine from neighboring Burgundian villages, such as Chambolle Musigny and Morey-Saint-Denis, have notable discernible differences. So, too, do Barolos from La Morra, Serralunga, Barolo, and Castiglione Falletto. They don't all taste the same any more than Pommard or Gevrey Chambertin taste the same.

La Morra has a number of excellent Barolo producers, all with wines that offer their own differing stylistic attributes. Even wines from two brothers with vineyards in the same village have their own characteristics. Renato and Giuliano Corino are La Morra growers. Until late 2005 they made wine together. For whatever reason, financial or philosophical, as of January 2006 they divided their property, which was previously their father's estate, into two separate properties. Renato's estate is in the Arborina area, approximately one km from the original winery, which now belongs to younger brother Giuliano. Giuliano kept the fabulous Giachini vineyard, and Renato took the equally fabulous, but different, Vignetto Rocche di Annunziata. They both make Barolo Normale and Barolo Arborina, dolcetto, and barbera.

Renato, who is five years older than Giuliano, is a powerful, striking-looking man with a quiet, confident, but not boastful or overbearing demeanor. His wines, even when from vineyards contiguous to those of his brother, are somewhat more forceful and bold, reflecting his strong personality. Giuliano, who is certainly not lacking in his own quiet charisma, makes wine that closely resembles him: a bit more complex and cerebral, featuring a bit more finesse and elegance, with its own sense of style. Giuliano's Barolo Giachini has for years been one of my favorites for its elegant, soft-for-Barolo, subtle style, with no lack of power. I'd liken it to a Chambolle Musigny or Morey-Saint-Denis 1er Cru in style and intensity, and I love those wines. Renato's much-sought-after Vignetto Rocche di Annunziata is completely different. It has an intoxicating, ethereal, unique, silky, seductive style that has depth, elegance, and finesse. Traditional Barolo flavors such as black cherry, rose petal, and Asian spices, tightly wrapped in a sinuous tannic spine, are found in the wine every vintage. But, honestly, descriptors don't do it justice.

Then there is Marco Marengo's fabulous Barolo Brunate, one of my longtime favorites. Brunate is one of the original single vineyards of Barolo. The vast majority of this cru is situated in the southeastern sector of La Morra, where some of the region's finest vineyards are found. Marengo's high-altitude vineyard is somewhere between 206 to 400 meters above sea level, with perfect south/southeast sun exposure. The vineyard has a complex soil mix consisting of clay and limestone, sand and pebbles. It can, and often does, produce some of the most fabulous and most complete wines in all of Barolo. A great Brunate can be a bit tough and off-putting when young, as it needs some bottle aging to show its stuff. But after some years in the bottle it will soften up and offer rare depth, subtle power, finesse, and intensity. Elio Altare, among others, likens this to the Burgundy Grand Cru Musigny. I very much love the Burgundian style of Marengo's wines.

There are many other growers in La Morra who make distinctive wine. There are similarities between their wines and other Barolos, of course, but there are obvious differences. Once you get to know the wines from differing regions, their qualities and characteristics, you can then decide which wine would go best with your dinner on a particular night.

Unlike the Burgundians, whom they should emulate in this, the Piedmontese have never clearly defined or legislated for any cru status for their tiny, highly diversified vineyards. There are no 1er Cru or Grand Cru designations for wines from even the most exalted vineyards. It would be nice to reward the vineyards with the best individual soils and microclimates. If a system of cru classification based on terroir were to be set up, à la Bourgogne, it would make life easier for everyone, growers and consumers alike. But I don't see it happening anytime soon, if ever. Politics.

When to Drink Piedmont Wines

The propitious moment to drink Piedmont wines is debatable and very personal. Some people believe that Barolos, etc. should be kept for a minimum of seven years after the vintage before being consumed. Ten or twenty years ago that was, correctly, the norm. The fact is, due to the recent fruit-driven, modern methods of vinification employed by many Piedmont winemakers, many of these wines can be enjoyed, with air, as soon as they are released, four/five years or so after the harvest. I have asked several Piedmont growers what they thought about when to drink their wine. Most regarded me quizzically and said, "It is subjective. If you want to taste the full fruit and youthful power of the wine, drink them young. If you prefer wines more complex rather than fruit driven, age them a while." That is a very true albeit rather simple answer to a complex question, and it pertains to other great wine regions as well, not just those from the Piedmont.

It is true that today many acclaimed modern Piedmont growers pick riper fruit than previous eras, age their wine in new and used oak barrels, bottle earlier, and strive for more supple, lower-acid wines. This often results in spectacular wines that are approachable early on but will age and develop for years. Even wines from "classic" vintages are often irresistible and fun to drink early on, *with several hours of decanting*. Of course, they will age and become more complex with time, like fine Bordeaux. Single-vineyard "crus" like San Rocco, Bricco Fiasco, Brunate, etc. do need more time than Barolo Normale. Generally, wines from warmer years, like 2007 and 2009, will be softer and more inviting sooner than those from colder years, like 2004, 2006, 2008, 2010, and 2013. But they are far from "soft." It's really a subjective decision as to when to try any wine. However, with Piedmont wines, patience is generally rewarded.

Azienda Agricola Azelia

Of all the wonderful Piedmont estates with whom I have done business, Azelia is the one that has reached the highest pinnacle of success. That's not to demean or diminish the accomplishments of any of the others who have all attained "star" status, but Azelia's star shines brightest.

Azelia's Barolo Bricco Fiasco vineyard is in Castiglione Falletto, and their Barolo San Rocco and Barolo Margheria vineyards are in Serralunga d'Alba. Their excellent Dolcetto d'Alba DOC Bricco dell'Oriolo is grown in the village of Montelupo Albese. They only have a total surface of about sixteen hectares of vineyards all combined.

It is actually odd and fortuitous that I was able to add Azelia to my portfolio. When Marc De Grazia invited me to visit him and meet with his growers over twenty years ago, I was initially hesitant. I then spoke not a word of Italian and was unsure of what wines he might have available for me that I would actually want. De Grazia already had three importers in Massachusetts at the time; why would he want or need a fourth? Marc said not to worry; there will be wine for you. OK, so I went, and I was blown away by what the other wholesalers left on the table, the best of them being Azelia. When I and the colleague I had with me tasted Azelia's wines, both he and I knew, these were must-buys.

Success in any field, whether it is in the wine industry or sports, does not come easily. Successful people strive to constantly improve, and the best never cease to work or rest on their laurels. Luigi Scavino, owner of Azelia, is a case in point. While their wines have always been exceptional, Luigi's scrupulous attention to detail, both in the vineyards and in making the wine, has paid off with Azelia being included among the upper echelon of Barolo producers. No one scored higher or made better wine than Azelia in the great 2010 Barolo vintage, maybe the best vintage ever for Barolo, and yet they only raised prices a modest 10 percent, and apologized for it.

Again, it is the hard work in the vineyards that has paid off. As I have said many times, great wine cannot be made without great grapes. To insure that they grow great grapes, Azelia generally has two green harvests. For them a green harvest is not just pruning back the vines. It is long, arduous, labor-intensive work that goes on for over a month during the warmest summer months. They inspect each bunch of grapes and cut out immature or unhealthy grapes that would sap the vine's strength and weaken the wine. Some years as much as 35 percent of the grapes, one-third of the crop, will be left on the ground. It is quite a sight to see, but this loss insures that the remaining grapes will ripen fully and attain maximum power.

All the work is done by hand, and only family members are allowed to prune the oldest, most venerable vines. This is dead-serious, backbreaking work but assures them of attaining the highest-quality grapes with a minimum of worries. The harvest, also, is totally by hand; no machines here. After picking, they do a very strict selection, examining every grape bunch in order to eliminate any berries deemed insufficient. While they, of course, lose a lot more grapes here too, this careful triage guarantees that only the best, healthiest grapes are used and, therefore, the best wine will be made. It is exhaustive work—I'm tired thinking about it—but it cannot be avoided if they are to maintain the high caliber of their wine. Vinification is kept as natural as possible, and the results speak for themselves.

As previously noted, the older generation of Barolo growers didn't understand how they could make more money by making better wine with far fewer grapes. It certainly blew the mind of Luigi's dad, Lorenzo. Fortunately, *Nono* Lorenzo reluctantly, shaking his head all the while, allowed his far-sighted son, Luigi, to go ahead and (gulp!) cut back. The new generation, like Luigi Scavino and his son, Lorenzo, do get it. Ironically, it is now Lorenzo, named after his grandfather, who is directing operations at the Azienda. You couldn't ask for a nicer family with whom to do business.

For Barolo, as with Burgundy, the grower and vineyard site are *more* important than the vintage. Also, as in Burgundy, advances in winemaking technology have aided the enlightened grower in difficult vintages. The quality level of recent Barolo vintages attests to that.

Where Baroli differ from Cru Burgundies is in pricing. Cru Baroli are *under*priced when one considers their high quality, flavor intensity, and the ageability of their wines. I have no doubt this pricing disparity will change in the future, as it has for all top growers, starting with the 2010 vintage.

Quoting Antonio Galloni, with whom I concur:

I am increasingly convinced that within the next ten to fifteen years the appreciation for Piedmont's top wines will explode globally as consumers become more familiar with the wines. Most of the very finest wines are made in small quantities of just a few hundred cases, so it is likely that prices will eventually have to catch up, even if that will take a while given the current state of the global economy. Readers with the financial resources to do so should take advantage of the current weakness in the market and the abundance of high quality vintages that are or soon will be available to build a collection of fine Barolo and Barbaresco at what very well might look like bargain prices in the future.

Gattinara

Antoniolo's Gattinara vineyards are located in the hills north of Barolo. In August of 2004 I drove from Barolo to Gattinara to visit the Antoniolo family. It took around an hour and a half driving very fast. This was the first time I walked their vineyards, and I was shocked at how small the area was. From a hill on the Antoniolo property, I could see all the Gattinara producers' vineyards and all the Antoniolo Crus.

Antoniolo's legendary Gattinaras are extraordinary wines that are similar to Barolo, as they, too, are produced entirely from the noble nebbiolo grape. They have a somewhat more "finesse" style, often with even greater complexity than Barolo. All Antoniolo's gorgeous Gattinaras are lively, sinewy, medium- to full-bodied, precise wines that are beautifully balanced and richly fruited, with penetrating precision. They have great flavor intensity, an intoxicating, fragrant bouquet of spring flowers and black cherries, with a long, lingering, spicy aftertaste. The sloped-hillside vineyards are planted in tough, rocky soil, where the grapes have to work to survive, which brings out their best. They have great aging potential, as their single-vineyard "crus" can live and improve for thirty-plus years. Their "Normal" bottling and nebbiolo "Juvenia" are wonderful 100 percent nebbiolo wines that have character, charm, and value.

While there are a few other people making Gattinara, Antoniolo is the most prestigious producer in the area, with, deservedly, the most renown. Current vintages of their wines are the best they have *ever* made, and that's really quite a statement. In the not-so-distant past, Gattinaras were overlooked and underrated Piedmont wines, but that has changed. Antoniolo's Gattinaras may have been under the radar in the past, but starting with the 2004 vintage even the most blasé critic and jaded wine lover have taken notice and given them their due. Their unobtainable 2005s were so good that Gambero Rosso rated Antoniolo as Italy's "Winery of the Year."

Barbaresco

If Barolo is considered the king of the Piedmont, Barbaresco is considered the queen. Like Barolo and Gattinara, Barbaresco is made with 100 percent nebbiolo grapes. Barbaresco vineyards are located in the Langhe, east of Alba, primarily in the communes of Barbaresco, Treiso, and Neive. Generally, they are similar to but somewhat warmer and softer than Barolos, with excellent aromatics and flavor intensity. There are various crus that while not inexpensive, offer value for the quality. The best-known Barbaresco producer is the enthusiastic, ubiquitous, mercurial, entrepreneurial, highly intelligent Angelo Gaja. He, more than anyone, is responsible for the reputation and renown of Barbaresco. Angelo's wines are not priced for those with cardiac problems, but excellent-quality Barbarescos that are more affordable can be found from Orlando Abrigo and Moccagatta as well as Castello di Verduno.

There has never been a better time to learn to love Piedmont wines. Current and future vintages are among the very best ever from this region. Prices of Burgundy and Bordeaux for comparable-quality wines are far higher. These are classic, world-class wines that will give pleasure for years to come.

Brunello di Montalcino

For a wine lover, it would be hard to beat a vacation in Tuscany. The green rolling hills are beautiful and seductive. The quaint, jewel-like tiny villages entice one to happily explore during the day. At night there are a number of interesting restaurants that serve delicious food along with wine that will not break the bank. The warmth of the people is unsurpassed anywhere. It is obvious that they care about you and are proud to serve you.

One of my favorite places to go in Tuscany is Montalcino, a small, medieval hilltop village located almost two thousand feet above sea level. Well situated, it is only around twenty miles from Siena and seventy from Florence. Going northeast of the village, it's heavily forested with dense woods and hilly terrain. You might just find a winery or two up there as well. The village itself is charming and fun to walk around, with more than a few wine shops. There are delightful inns and B and Bs, many on the properties of some Brunello di Montalcino producers, that are affordable and comfortable. I love visiting there, enjoying the hospitality, food, and wine of the region, as well as seeing some of the growers with whom I do business.

Mocali

Of course, the main claim to fame for Montalcino is that the region produces some of Italy's most famous and sought-after wine. After a strong recommendation at Vinitaly from a Tuscan producer with whom I was doing business, I sought out Alessandra and Tiziano Ciacci and tried their wine. Twenty-plus years later I am still annually offering new vintages of their wonderful Mocali wines from Montalcino, along with others from Morellino di Scansano.

The first time Bonnie and I visited Mocali we were staying in Castenuovo Berardenga, about an hour away from Montalcino, in Chianti. We had no appointment; we just went on the spur of the moment. We followed the directions we received at the large wine shop on the hill as you enter Montalcino, but soon it appeared that we were lost. We went down a dirt road that seemed to lead nowhere. Was it the right one? Turning around was not an option. Finally, after what seemed a very long time, the Azienda loomed in front of us. Fortunately, the lovely, charming Alessandra and quiet, stoic Tiziano were there to warmly greet us, and there *was* space to turn around.

From day one I have been a fan of Mocali's full-bodied but elegant red wines: Brunello di Montalcino, Rosso di Montalcino, as well as the two different Morellino di Scansanos, which come from property passed down to Alessandra from her family. But it was their beautifully packaged, 100 percent organic Tuscan olive oil that caught Bonnie's eye on this trip. After tasting it smeared on some bread, we soon began importing that too.

Campo di Marzo

It is such a small world. Some years back I was unexpectedly introduced to the wines of Tiziano Ciaci's younger brother, Fabiano. One of our friends went to Montalcino and met Fabiano and his beautiful wife, Valentina, at their property, Campo di Marzo. They fell in love with the wine and the family and invited the couple and their young kids to stay for a week at their home in Lexington, just a few miles from my house. We were invited to dinner, where we met the couple and tried their wines—Brunello and Rosso di Montalcino, among others. We have been buyers of Campo di Marzo wines ever since.

Analogous to Renato and Giuliano Corino's situation in the La Morra, Fabiano and Tiziano split their estate in half for tax purposes and philosophical differences. The property dates back to the 1900s and was started by their great-grandfather, Savino. In 1952 their granddad Dino bought the Mocali property from the Count di Argiano. His son, their father, Silvano, ran the farm in the 1970s. Fabiano and Tiziano are still good friends and have no problem working beside one another with no animosity at all—to the contrary. We do business with both Ciacci families, quite happily.

Uccelliera

Andrea Cortenesi is one of my favorite growers. We go back to the beginning, when I first started importing Italian wines and when he had not yet received any recognition for his wines. Andrea, whose Brunello di Montalcino is now ranked with Siro Pacente, Casanova di Neri, and Valdicava as one of the upper-echelon Brunellos, is just as warm, welcoming, and nice now as he was when first I met him twenty-plus years ago. He always gives me a big hug and a happy smile. He was born and raised in Montalcino and has worked in Montalcino's wine world all his life. Like the Ciacci brothers, Tiziano and Fabiano, he has never had it easy.

Uccelliera is a miniscule gem of a domaine located in the warm southern Castelnuovo dell'Abate part of the Montalcino zone. In the mid-1980s, by virtue of hard work, scrimping, and saving, Andrea purchased the property from the renowned Ciacci-Piccolomini family, for whom he consulted. He worked for years renewing the vineyards. Recently he added two hectares adjacent to Ciacci's famous Pianrosso vineyard and now has six hectares under vines. By using advanced vinification techniques, he makes absolutely brilliant wine. Uccelliera is consistently among the stars of Brunello. I love Andrea, and his wines are fabulous.

In the past, when we would have lunch at Andrea's farm, in their small, very modest kitchen, his ninety-year-old mother was the one who did the cooking. She wouldn't have it any other way, and the food was always better than good. I learned a tremendous amount about Montalcino wines from Andrea as we rode around looking at his vineyards. I knew that the sangiovese grown in Montalcino differed somewhat from sangiovese grown in Chianti, as it is a different strain of the grape *sangiovese grosso*, but I didn't know that there were many different clonal varieties. Andrea told me he had seven different types planted that he blended in his wine to add flavor and complexity. Sangiovese grosso, which is used exclusively in Montalcino, has more loosely bunched grapes than the smaller, sangiovese piccolo. One strain of sangiovese grosso is actually called "Brunello," which means, "little brown one" in Italian, so named because of the brown hue of its skin. That is the grape that gives Brunello di Montalcino wines their power and ageability.

It is wise to look for Rossos di Montalcino from top Montalcino producers when on wine lists, or at a shop, as they are very often excellent values. Many are just declassified Brunello. Legally, Brunello di Montalcino must be kept for four years before release, and for two of those years they are obliged to be kept in wood. The growers always need cashflow. There are, inevitably, parts of vineyards that are weaker than some others, possibly due to positioning or the age of the vines. Grapes from these are often used in the blending of Rossos di Montalcino, which may be somewhat lighter and readier to drink than their big brothers but can also be delicious. Mocali, Campo di Marzo, and Uccelliera all make terrific Rosso di Montalcino.

Umbria

Antonelli—Umbria—Montefalco

Filippo Antonelli is a count, but he will never tell you that. Filippo, who I would guess to be in his late forties, is not very tall and not overly distinctive looking at first glance. After conversing with him for a while, listening to his speech, phrasing, and articulation, a different opinion starts to form. The sparkle in his dark eyes, the quick wit and sly grin quickly show that this is a different breed of cat. Filippo walks with an Italian *insouciance*, forgive the French word. It's a kind of boneless, I don't care, I am comfortable in my skin and it doesn't matter to me what you think, kind of walk that only an aristocrat could pull off. It is not learned; it comes from breeding. And yet Filippo is a down-to-earth, unexpectedly fun guy that I like and admire.

The Antonelli estate, located in Umbria, more specifically, Montefalco, is vast and they don't just grow grapes, but those are what most interest me. Sangiovese and the white grechetto grapes are grown in the area, but Montefalco is renowned for its indigenous grape variety, sagrantino, which isn't found anywhere else. Sagrantino supposedly has the highest tannin content of any known grape variety in the world. The name was said to have been derived from the Latin word for "sacrament," which makes some sense, as it was originally cultivated by monks thousands of years ago. In the 1960s, however, the grape nearly disappeared and was eventually brought back to life thanks to the work of a few dedicated winemakers, like Filippo. Since 1981, area wine producers have joined together in the Montefalco Consortium, enforcing production standards while promoting their wines around the globe. A distinctive and complex wine, sagrantino has grown in popularity over time. Today, the total wine production of sagrantino is one million bottles per year. The DOCG label was obtained in 1992.

The most powerful wine that Antonelli makes is their Sagrantino di Montefalco DOCG Chiusa di Pannone. It is produced from grapes grown in the enclosed small Pannone hillside vineyard. The wine has received many deserved awards over the years. Their 2004 is one of the most concentrated, tannic wines I have ever tried, but it is undeniably great. If it still exists in someone's cellar today, that person is fortunate. I wish I still had some.

Antonelli's Baiocco Umbria Rosso is less expensive and has received high praise from Italy's top wine periodical, *Gambero Rosso*. However, often my favorite Antonelli wine, price to quality, is their Montefalco Rosso Riserva, which is usually a blend of approximately 70 percent sangiovese, 15 percent sagrantino, and 15 percent merlot. Each varietal is vinified separately, by gravity with maceration and fermentation in contact with the skins for fourteen days, at 25°C. Malolactic fermentation takes place. The wine clarifies spontaneously with no need for filtration. This is yummy stuff and very inexpensive for the quality. It would be terrific with any Italian dishes, grilled fare, and even roast chicken. Antonelli's Sagrantino di Montefalco Passito is a supersweet wine that would pair well with all chocolate dishes.

Vacation in Umbria

Here's something to know about Montefalco in general and the Antonelli property in particular: it would be a *great*, inexpensive place to go for a vacation. I have stayed there and have sent others, who have come back raving about the place. It is relaxing and beautiful on the farm and, not far away, there are some fabulous restaurants, many with extensive, inexpensive wine lists. Filippo says that Umbria, and especially Montefalco, can offer a genuine experience for its visitors. "Although our atmosphere is similar to Tuscany, Umbria is less crowded, less expensive, less spread out—and truly authentic," he says. "Most importantly, we enjoy sharing our unique winemaking approach with guests and demonstrating the essential role that Sagrantino wine plays in the region's culture and history."

Umbria is a very lush area that some call "Italy's green heart." Sometimes overshadowed by its better-known, somewhat more glamorous neighbor, Tuscany, Umbria is nevertheless a beautiful, tranquil area that is well worth visiting. There are lots of things to do and see, including the walled medieval hamlet of Montefalco. There are idyllic, sleepy villages close by to visit and explore. The gently sloping hills and vineyards are enticing to see with many of the wineries happy to welcome tourists with open arms. It's only thirty or so miles from Perugia, and even going off to Tuscany is easily doable. I drove to Florence from Umbria on one stay. How I got there, even with GPS, is still a mystery. But with the help of several friendly people who didn't laugh, cops included, I made it.

Verona

I know that many travelers who have been to Italy share my sentiments when I say, "I love Italy." I love the warmth of the people, their language, their openness and energy. I love the beautiful countryside, from the Piedmont to Calabria, and I especially love their food and wine diversity. I have been to Rome two or three times and Florence many more than that, but the northern city of Verona is my favorite. Verona is not very large, encompassing only 550 square miles and under 300,000 inhabitants. It is located on the Adige River, with excellent, not overly expensive restaurants on both sides of the river. There are lots of neat shops and friendly, interesting, busy people, all of which in and of itself makes Verona a great vacation destination.

I have been there dozens of times, as the wine fair known as Vinitaly takes place annually in Verona in late March/early April. Vinitaly is the most important wine fair in Italy, and it is a huge undertaking featuring the very best and worst of Italian wine, as well as international offerings from everywhere in the wine world. For me, it has been obligatory, as all my Italian growers will be gathered in one place, giving me a cost-effective opportunity to try the new vintages and new releases. In addition, it gives me the freedom to look for new producers, if I so desire.

For many years I went to Verona just for the wine fair, kept my nose down, and worked hard, oblivious to the charm of the city. One year I asked Bonnie if she wanted to come. "We could take the train to Venice afterward," I said coaxingly. "It's only an hour and a half away." "Why not?" she said in agreement.

I had always stayed at a hotel, now out of business, that was recommended to me by the De Grazias. Very well located near the square, but very spartan, it was just off the main street and was exceedingly noisy, but I didn't really mind. The room was tiny and the shower so miniscule that a larger man than I would have had trouble getting in to shut the door. However, I was so tired after the long day of work, plus the wining and dining with growers, that I was inured to it. Most of us spent our evenings after dinner at the Bottega del Vino, a wine bar/restaurant of international repute; there is one in New York. We looked forward to discussing the day's events and talking "wine" while we sampled and compared glasses of great wine from their voluminous offerings, often while out the door in the street.

I always got to bed far later than I would have liked, as I had to get up very early to get to the fair and do it all over again. When Bonnie and I arrived at our hotel, and she saw how run-down and poorly managed the hotel was, she couldn't quite believe it. It's true, the bath towels were as thin as dishtowels, and the bed was not overly comfortable. It didn't take long for her to go down the street and find us an infinitely better hotel, the Gabbia d'Oro (Golden Cage). Management there was warm, efficient, and friendly, and while the room she secured was not large, it was comfortable and had a bathtub. Big difference.

The next day I went off to work at the Vinitaly fair, as usual, and Bonnie explored the city. Of course, she did some shopping as well. When I came back that evening, she asked me if I had ever gone around the city. "No, not really," I replied. She said that we should take an extra day for me to finally get to see it before we went off to Venice. It would be well worth the time, as Verona was "neat." OK, no argument from me.

Unbeknownst to me previously, Verona is one of the main tourist destinations in northern Italy. It has a strong artistic heritage, as three of Shakespeare's plays were set in Verona: *Romeo and Juliet*, *The Two Gentlemen of Verona*, and *The Taming of the Shrew*. The city has been awarded World Heritage Site status by UNESCO because of its unique urban structure and architecture. And they have several fairs and shows annually, with the highlight, perhaps, being the world-famous operas that take place every summer in the Arena, an ancient Roman amphitheater. Again, I had been oblivious to it all.

One of Verona's main must-see attractions is "Juliet's house" (la casa di Giulietta). This house dates from the thirteenth century, and the family coat of arms can still be seen on the wall. The balcony itself, which overlooks the courtyard, was only added in the twentieth century, which doesn't seem to concern the hordes of young girls who flock to it every year, gazing down, hoping to find their Romeo.

Inside the house there is a small museum, and in the courtyard there is a bronze sculpture of Juliet. People rub her now slightly worn right breast for luck, as did I. It's fascinating to see the many love notes stuck on the walls and doors in the entrance to the courtyard. Wherefore art thou Romeo, indeed?

If I had never taken Bonnie with me, I would no doubt have missed it all.

Soave

Unfortunately for them, quality Soave producers have an even harder time convincing people to buy their wines than Chablis growers. It's not that their name was stolen, à la Chablis and Champagne. It is just that in the past so much bland, at best, plonk was made with lowland-grown trebbiano, which was then sold under the Soave brand name. That created an unfair, uphill battle for the handful of industrious, caring growers who do make exceptional wine, primarily from the garganega grape, which has distinctive character, style, and grace.

As the Soave zone is only a short trip outside of the city of Verona, it's not hard for me to go there when I attend Vinitaly. Most of the best vineyards are situated in the eastern part, high up on the hills, north of the highway, on the Verona-Venezia road. I have more than once walked these very steep, often muddy, hills, so I know first-hand how hard these vineyard sites are to work.

Monte Tondo

Hardworking Gino Magnabosco, third-generation owner of Monte Tondo, is justly proud of the quality of his wines. He has twenty-five hectares of vineyard sites on well-drained volcanic soils that are among the best plots to be found in the DOC Soave zone. They are Monte Tenda, Monte Foscarino, and Monte Tondo, the last of which they have adopted for their name. Gino is a wonderful, honest, literally down-to-earth man who is constantly striving for perfection in the vineyard and the *chais*. When I first met this very short, kind of stubby, fiftyish-plus man with gnarled hands and weathered features, he said to me, "Look at my hands," as he held out a pair of good-sized mitts à la Yogi Berra. "All I care about is working my vineyards and producing the finest quality wine of which I am capable." You've got to love it. His Monte Tondo Soave Classico is one of a handful of Soaves made from 100 percent garganega grapes, which are grown on their own well-placed hillside vineyards. I loved their wines from when I first tasted them some years back.

Traditionally their Soave Classico is a brilliant green/gold in color, with a lovely floral bouquet, crisp on the palate with subtle flavors of peach, citrus, and hazelnuts. But Monte Tondo makes an entire range of wines, from sparkling to dessert, and it is all good. Several have deservedly received high praise and excellent marks from *Wine Spectator* and *Wine Advocate*. They also received this high accolade from Gambero Rosso, Italy's foremost wine guide: "Gino Magnabosco is the perfect incarnation of the strong-willed farmer who never gives up, works untiringly and has plenty of experience. There is a vision of the future behind his straightforward spontaneity. All that effort and passion are not wasted. Fortunately, the rewards come in high-quality wines that Gino often releases at very reasonable prices."

Their best wine is their single vineyard, slightly wood-aged Casette Foscarin, which is deep and complex with very surprising ageability. We bought too much of it one vintage. It is never a fast seller here, unfortunately. We were amazed at how well it kept and how complex it became. Of course, we would have preferred that it were aged in someone else's cellar, but the lesson was learned and almost worth it. We never have lost a bottle.

I have always been impressed by Monte Tondo's very fair pricing for the quality. And I loved Gino Magnabosco and his perky, intelligent business partner and daughter, Marta, from the outset. They both have great energy and passion. And since I, too, am vertically challenged at five feet six inches or so, they make me feel like a king. Marta is maybe five feet tall, with Gino only slightly taller. But they are giants in their field, and they have my utmost respect.

California

Mount Eden Vineyards

A few years after I started my import company, I decided to expand and add some California wines to the portfolio. One of my customers who had become a friend, J. P. Miller, had just moved out to California. J. P. was kind enough to offer to take me to some wineries that he thought might be a good fit for me. You cannot imagine the pleasant shock and surprise I felt when he set me up with an appointment at the iconic Mount Eden Vineyards. I was well aware of who they were and knew MEV to be a gem. I called Ellie Paterson, who took care of the business side of the operation, and fixed a time to meet.

Ellie and I had a very friendly meeting over a glass of their wine, and she explained that she would like to have me represent her wines in Massachusetts. I could hardly keep a straight face and hide my exultation. The current Massachusetts distributor with whom she had been doing business had dual licensing as both a wholesaler and a retailer but was only interested in selling the MEV Estate Chardonnay, and primarily retail. They were not particularly interested in supplying the wine to other accounts, but I was. Ellie wanted statewide distribution and balanced orders that included their old-vines cabernet and pinot noir. I tried the current examples of their wine and was more than happy with them. No problem. Ellie cut me a fabulous deal on some ridiculously good old-vine cabernet sauvignon, and we were off to the races. For me, having Mount Eden Vineyards in my portfolio was a coup.

Located at an elevation of two thousand feet on Santa Cruz Mountain, overlooking the Silicon Valley, Mount Eden Vineyards is a world unto itself. A cautionary note if ever you go there: people who are afraid of heights or who suffer from vertigo need to forget about it and stay home. To get to the winery, one must travel a two-mile winding, narrow dirt road that seems endless. I am told part is now repaved. Just finding the road to get up there can be interesting, as it incongruously starts in the middle of a placid suburban neighborhood. I passed it by the first time, and I am sure I won't be the last to have missed it. Once you get up there, though, the view from their steep vineyards is breathtaking.

Mount Eden's vineyards were started by the legendary Martin Ray in the late 1940s, and he used Corton Charlemagne clones when planting the Estate Chardonnay. Handsome, blonde, and blue-eyed, quietly self-effacing but totally self-confident, Jeff Patterson has been the winemaker since 1983. He and Ellie are now the majority owners. It is not easy for them to turn a profit and make ends meet each year, because the yields from these high-altitude vineyards are ridiculously low. There are only four thousand cases of Estate wine produced in a good year. Jeff says, "Typically we get between one to two tons per acre, and usually that's on the low end." Most Napa or Sonoma vineyards often double that yield. The microclimate so high up is very cold, with a cutting wind from Monterey Bay. This helps insure low production, but that is not all. Walking the vineyard clearly shows why production is so low, as it's easy to see: there is practically no topsoil. What they have is only mostly just a thin veneer on top of mostly rock and shale. "Effectively, we don't have much soil, at least as most people think of soil," says Jeff.

I love Mount Eden's wines, which are all great, but I have a special fondness for their Estate Chardonnay. My wife, Bonnie, loves it, and for her sixtieth birthday party that was the white wine we served to guests who were celebrating with us. I, personally, know of no other California chardonnay that has the same characteristics and qualities as does Mount Eden's Estate Chardonnay. As with all quality wines, there are always some variations from vintage year to vintage year, but almost always this is a white wine that can age and improve for years. Did I mention the Corton Charlemagne clones? No, it really doesn't taste 100 percent French but, when young, it has the deep intensity, crisp acid balance, and tremendously supportive spine of very crisp acidity with, perhaps, unexpected minerality. Like a Corton Charlemagne when young, it too can benefit from being decanted.

I am offering a quote from Antonio Galloni, who in his "Vinous" edition wrote about the 2011 MEV Estate Chardonnay. There is no way I could describe this wine better than he has here: "Mount Eden's 2011 Chardonnay is simply magnificent. Intense and tightly-coiled from the very first taste, the 2011 pulsates with energy, texture and pure class. Bright citrus, lemon oil, flowers and crushed rocks are all vivid in the glass, but it is the wine's exceptional balance that stands out most. The long, vibrant finish is a thing of beauty."

The fact is Mount Eden Vineyards is a treasure of a California winery. Everything they produce is of quality and offers value. And what they do offer is the exact opposite of mass-produced plonk at whatever price.

A Barbecue at Rancho Sisquoc — Santa Maria Valley

I have always loved visiting Rancho Sisquoc. The property, located in northern Santa Barbara County, dates back to 1852, when it was a Mexican land grant. It was named by the Chumash Indians, who called the area "Sisquoc," meaning "gathering place." It was purchased in 1952 by James Flood of San Francisco. The Floods have never lived on the property but do visit a few times a year. Ed Holt and his wife, Mary, solid, pragmatic Missourians, have been managing the property as if it were their own since 1987. They do live there and have raised their now-grown kids on the ranch. Their daughter, Sarah Holt Mullins, is now the current winemaker, after having completed her enological studies and stints working at various wineries.

The winery is just a small fraction of this 37,000-acre working ranch. Cattle and horses are run, vegetables are grown, and minerals are mined in addition to the growing of several different grape varieties. Rancho Sisquoc is a great place to grow grapes, as their vineyards are warmer than those in lower Santa Maria Valley and cooler than ones in the Santa Ynez Valley twenty miles to the south. That is due to the transverse range of coastal mountains that run west to east and bring cool winds and fog inland from the Pacific Ocean.

Rancho Sisquoc's wines were first recommended to me by the ever personable, highly intelligent Randall Graham, then owner of Bonny Doon Vineyards. Many years back, I was looking to add some California properties to my wholesale portfolio and asked Randall for some recommendations. Randall and I became friendly from the time I gambled by buying twenty-five cases of his first vintage of the then unknown Rhône -Ranger blend Le Cigar Volant 1984.

Usually, when going to California, I would fly into LAX, rent a car and drive two hours to Rancho Sisquoc to spend two days there. I would then wend my way up the 101 to Paso Robles, see some growers, then go to Santa Cruz Mountain, where I would visit both Cinnabar Vineyards and Mount Eden Vineyards. The next day I would end up in Healdsburg, where I would be based for a few days. I would have appointments to visit the many Sonoma winemakers with whom I was doing business. This was easy, far easier than in France, as they are all very close to one another, none more than an hour away by car. I always enjoy Healdsburg, as it is a charming, somewhat quaint rustic town that abounds with excellent, fairly priced restaurants. And, yes, I do happily drink California wines when in California. This year, however, I had to start off doing the reverse by flying into San Francisco and leaving from LA. There had been severe and dangerous forest fires in the Santa Barbara area, with a prodigious amount of nearly toxic smoke.

Although I usually traveled alone, this year I decided to take my then–retail store manager with me, Paul Tag. Paul was in his early fifties, six feet one inch tall, and he weighed a rock solid two hundred pounds. I didn't feel I needed a bodyguard, but he qualified. Paul had never been to California, let alone to wineries to taste. Our first stop was actually at the offices of Marty Bannister for a tasting of her current releases. Marty, who founded Vinquiry, a company that provides high-quality technical service to the wine industry, made a small amount of chardonnay, pinot noir, and zinfandel. It was a tiny, boutique operation, and her wines—which she, unfortunately, no longer makes—were pristine. We started off with her delicious chardonnay, which typically was crystalline and pure, with slightly exotic citrus flavors of mango, orange, and lime. As usual, it was nearly 14 percent ABV, not hot but with plenty of punch. I, of course, tasted and used a spit bucket. We went through her whole range, with pinot noir next, then zinfandel. After we tried the chard, I noticed that Paul was not spitting. I mentioned this to him, and he said, "Oh, this wine is too good to spit." OK, I thought. You are an adult, do what you will. I didn't say anything, as it really didn't matter. I did 100 percent of the driving.

We went through the day visiting a number of properties, and after stopping at our motel to shower and change, we went to a bistro very close by that had been highly recommended. It was a small, funky place, Ralph's Bistro, I think it was called, that was down-to-earth and fun. We liked our waitress, and the food looked imaginative but not weird. I spotted a Pezzi King Old Vines Zinfandel on the list, and as I distributed their wine in Massachusetts, gladly ordered it. It was very rich, not jammy, but with powerful raspberry flavors with black pepper overlaid and a seamless 14.9 percent alcohol by volume. Although we had been tasting all day, I *always* spit, never drink, so I was as fresh as a daisy. I assumed Paul was OK too. Faulty assumption. When he was late the next morning—we always leave early—I became concerned and perturbed. When he finally made an appearance, he was hung over, with a green tinge and a nasty headache. He said, "Joel, I am not going to drink another drop of wine on this trip." It seemed that he had learned his lesson. But I must be a bad person, because I must admit: I was somewhat amused.

When we finally made our way back south to Rancho Sisquoc, the forest fires were out, and while there was still a bit of smoke smell in the air, it wasn't off-putting. The first thing always Ed does, once we settle into one of the bunkhouses, is to take us out in some sort of four-wheel-drive vehicle to show off the new vineyard work that he has done since I was last there. It's always fun and informative. Ed could have been a bodyguard too. He isn't quite as tall as Paul, but he is bulkier, and not much of it was fat. He and Mary are great caretakers of that property, and it was a lucky thing for both the Holts and Floods that they found each other.

Ed and Mary informed us that we would be going to a barbecue that night at the line shack where the cowboys bunked. They had a number of invited guests, one of whom was a chef who specialized in this type of cooking. "Great," I said, "we're in." Ed told us, "You know, it might get cold out there tonight, as we will be outside, so dress accordingly." OK, I thought, I'll just bring a few layers to leave in the car that I can put on if it does get cold. Paul, ever the contrarian, said, "I have an old Seagram's Cocktail windbreaker, and that should be fine." OK, whatever.

We headed out in Ed's four-wheel-drive extended pickup. We really needed four-wheel drive, as we went through two or three running brooks and all around rough terrain. Although the line shack wasn't that far as the crow flies, the route we needed to take to get there was circuitous and slow.

When we finally arrived, there were twelve to fourteen people already there, and the barbeque pit was fired up. I was told that "the judge" and his wife would be coming and that he was a "nice guy" but that she was difficult.

I loved it out there in the middle of nowhere, with the stars just starting to glimmer and the smell of the fire to entice. There were a number of Rancho Sisquoc wines, but others had brought an array of diverse bottlings, and I was happily sampling my way through. Someone had put on an Andrea Bocelli's *Romanza* CD, and it was blasting forth. I loved that too. Then the judge arrived, a younger man than I had expected. His wife was much younger too. True to form, she objected to the Bocelli CD and wanted some cowboy music. This was disconcerting to most, as we were happy to keep things as they were. Then someone asked me, as an out-of-town guest of the ranch, how I felt about it. I retorted immediately, "I think Andrea Bocelli is *great*." Sorry, judge's wife, but that settled that.

I very much enjoyed the diverse offerings of barbeque served, and I thoroughly enjoyed the wines, also diverse. The people were interesting and a lot of fun, even the judge. I had a great time. Need I say, as the evening progressed so did the cold, which just seeped into your bones. I kept adding layers as the night wore on, and I was fine. When I finally caught up to Paul, in his faded, puke-green Seagram's windbreaker, he was shivering, all six feet of him. Just as I noticed his suffering, so did one of the other guests. "Man," he said, "you're freezing." Slipping off his Rancho Sisquoc sweatshirt, as he was Paul's size, he said, "Take this; they'll give me another one. You need it more than I do." I never took Paul on another trip, and I don't think he would have gone if I had offered.

When I sent Mary Holt, at Rancho Sisquoc, what I had written about the barbecue she wrote back, "Dear Joel, Oh the fun we had!!! Do you remember the jumping fish on our way home that night?" I actually didn't, until she reminded me. When we left the barbecue, around midnight, there was a full moon. All of us, including Paul, who had by now warmed up, were satiated with wine and food, contented and euphoric. Going back at night over the rough terrain, which made us happy for the moonlight, was a lot trickier than when we left during the day. Ed, of course, knew the property like the back of his hand and was very used to tooling around at night in a four-wheel-drive vehicle.

As mentioned previously, there were three swiftly running creeks to cross to get back to the ranch. At each one, I don't know if it was feeding time for the fish or what, but as soon as our headlights hit the water as we were going across, hundreds of silver fish started jumping like crazy. In that setting, with the moonlight, it was surreal, just an amazing sight.

Randall Grahm

The iconoclastic Randall Grahm has to be one of the greatest characters in the wine world. He got into wine after graduating from University of California at Santa Cruz. Legend has it that he was working at a Beverly Hills wine shop where he was accorded the opportunity to taste a goodly number of wines, many of them great and most of them French. After that it was see you later; he was another poor fish hooked by the wine bug.

He went back to school, this time at UC–Davis, where he got a degree in plant sciences in 1979. I first became aware of Randall's existence only when I was shown a bottle of his first vintage of Le Cigare Volant 1984. Back then I was into science fiction, French, and wine so I was intrigued by the bottle and captivated by the wine. If memory serves me right, it sold for $36 wholesale a case on a twenty-five-case drop deal, the same price as Jacques Reynaud's 1983 Côtes du Rhône Châteaux de Fonsalette. I could deal it down to $3.99 a bottle, and did. I had very good success with the wine, so when I had the opportunity to meet Randall at his home on Santa Cruz Mountain, where he had his first vineyard, I went.

When I first met Randall, he was surprisingly reserved and very cordial. At this stage of my life, I was definitely into French wines and regarded all but very few California wines with suspicion. I well remember first tasting Randall's chardonnay from his vineyard just outside the door to his house. I even have a photo of me up there, uncharacteristically taking copious notes. I was surprised and very impressed with Randall's chardonnay. It was not unlike Mount Eden Vineyard's chard: deeply colored, rich, but elegantly light on its feet despite the power. I don't know the vintage or remember the price; most likely there was not much to be had. But I well remember what I said to Randall, seriously and without a trace of condescension: "This is quite good." Randall simply and sincerely said, "Thank you."

Once I found out that his cellar was comprised of nearly 100 percent great French wines, Burgs in particular, we became fast friends. He came out to the shop one year just before Thanksgiving and actually worked with me the day before Thanksgiving, helping people with wine selections. I'll never forget when a little old lady went over to him for help making a choice. After he guided her she said, "Well, how do I know what you are selling me is good?" He looked down from his six-foot-three or so height, kind of went hmmph, and said, "Lady, I am a winemaker." I think she was sufficiently cowed, and I had a good laugh.

On another occasion when I went to visit him, prior to arriving we stopped at the side of the road, in a rather gravelly but isolated area, to get some relief from the long car ride. When I got out, not realizing that the tiny pebbles over hard rock were not stable, I slipped and fell forward, scraping my hands and wounding my pride. It wasn't a big deal until we got to Randall's house. Exuberant and irrepressible as always, he was all excited to see me. If he were a dog he would have been wagging his tail like crazy. He ran up, and with all two-hundred-plus pounds of him, slapped me a five so hard that it brought tears to my eyes.

We have pretty much lost contact over the years, but I still have great affection and admiration for him and have been very pleased for all of his successes.

Trip to California

Not all my buying trips were to France and Italy. I annually went to California too. Back in the mid-1980s, one of the owners of a medium-sized Boston-based import company invited me to accompany him and two of his sales staff on a trip to California. His company was one of my major retail suppliers, and they were going to visit a number of producers with whom I did business.

It was an invitation not expected to be taken seriously, as he and I had a mostly rocky relationship. I wasn't his favorite person, nor was he mine. We had been conversing on the phone about a tightly allocated California wine that I coveted and usually bought, which had been sold out from under me. I was not happy as, apparently, no more was to be had. Tongue in cheek he said, "Look, I am going to California next Monday for a week to see all of our major suppliers including this one. Why don't you come? Maybe then we can get you the wine." I said, "Maybe I will." I thought about it for a while and decided that if I could get a reasonably priced ticket, then yes, I would go. It could be beneficial and was sure to be educational and, quite possibly, fun. I called my travel agent, locked in a ticket, and called the company and told the owner, let's call him "Bobby," that I was in. He must have fallen off his chair but accepted the fact that I was going graciously.

It was to be an interesting trip, as we were to start in Napa and Sonoma and wend our way south outside of Santa Barbara. I really liked the two salesmen who were on the trip. They were fun guys, down-to-earth and knowledgeable. Once we landed, Bobby and I continued our strained relationship in the car, neither of us overly pleased with the other. However, once we settled in and got to actually know each other a bit better, we became friendly, and the tension eased up. I was, after all, a major customer of his company. Bobby was a highly intelligent, complex individual—somewhat high-strung in nature, but he could be very funny in a sardonic/sarcastic way, depending on the context. Once we cleared the air, we laughed a lot.

When we got to Napa, I was blown away by where we were staying, a beautiful house on the property of a famous winery on the Silverado Trail. The place was beyond gorgeous, and we had it entirely to ourselves. When we went inside to settle in, we found bedrooms on two floors. There was a large master bedroom that overlooked the vineyard, with a few other bedrooms on either side. I actually liked best a bedroom on the first floor that had a great view and looked to be very comfortable and was conveniently placed. I now knew how Bobby's mind worked. I went up to the master bedroom and said, "This one's for me." Bobby, as I expected, said, "Oh no. I get that one." "OK, fine," I said, smothering a grin. "Then I'll take the bedroom below."

Lunch with the Legendary, Charismatic Joe Heitz

We visited many different growers, tasted a lot of good wine, and had some good food on this trip. All of it was beneficial and educational, even if I couldn't get any of the wine I wanted. It was fun too. However, the most memorable visit for me was when we went to see the legendary, irascible Joe Heitz.

Joe got into wine in the '40s. After working as a cellar man, he went to UC–Davis and earned a master's degree in enology. He worked for a while with revered winemaker André Tchelistcheff at Beaulieu Vineyard. In 1961 Joe bought an eight-acre vineyard south of St. Helena and in 1964 purchased a 160-acre vineyard property on Spring Valley. Joe began to focus on cabernet sauvignon. In 1966 he teamed up with Tom May, who owned a vineyard in Oakville. In 1966, from grapes grown in Tom's vineyard, they produced a cabernet sauvignon that was so extraordinary that from then on it was designated on the label as "Martha's Vineyard." No one in Napa had previously placed a vineyard designation on their wine. I well remember Heitz 1968 and 1970 Martha's Vineyard cabernet sauvignons. The argument back then was over which was better, Heitz Martha's or BV's George de la Latour cabernet sauvignons. They were remarkably rich wines that gave Classified Growth Bordeaux more than a little competition, qualitatively. Rich and powerful, with flavors of blackberry and cedar, they oozed finesse.

The afternoon that we had lunch with Joe was sunny, warm, and bright. The temperature was somewhere in the low seventies, and there was no humidity. A perfect California day. We were seated outside, and the setting was lovely. I had seen Joe only once before, when he was giving a talk on his wine and wine in general. He was a big man, larger than life, with an imposing speaking style. Joe was highly intelligent, very opinionated but very knowledgeable. He most certainly was charismatic, and he knew it. During lunch, we were trying various vintages of Heitz wines and Joe, who was the opposite of shy, was extolling their virtues, using many adjectives and descriptors. I was kind of amused by his style and bombast. After a while, he turned to me and asked, "So, what do you think of my wines?" I must have been in a silly mood, because I immediately and reflexively mimicked him and parroted his exact phrases, gently mocking him by using the same intonation as he. He looked at me, stunned, and took the cork he was holding, let it fly, and bounced it off my head. I guess I struck a nerve. I started laughing and said, "Well, Joe, I always wanted to own a vineyard in the Napa Valley." At that he cracked up too.

Some Additional Interesting Dining Experiences

One may assume that I always have wonderful meals with great bottles of wine when I travel, but nothing could be further from the truth. My memorable experiences that were positive have been gleaned from an over thirty-year span. Trust me, most of the meals I have had on wine-buying trips are forgettable. While lunch is obligatory, time is of the essence, so often it's at fast-serving upscale truck stops or local eateries. Good, or not so good, hearty food is served but not worth remembering. In the past few years, I have noticed better options, healthier food, more imaginatively prepared, but that is a recent phenomenon.

As noted, we do try to dine better at night, as that is our reward for working hard for many hours all day, but we rarely order wine that turns out to be exciting. Shocking? Here's why. We invariably want to try wines from unknown producers or from someone whose wines we haven't tried in a while. This empirical testing is expensive and necessary and, unfortunately, very rarely do we ever come up with winners. I frankly cannot remember a single one that was worth following through with and importing. Too often it is bland, over oaked or stripped wine that is overpriced and boring. I know; why do we do it? We are always trying to catch lightning in a bottle.

Sometimes we are permitted to bring in samples of wine picked up at growers' cellars to try later. If so allowed, we usually still buy something off the list to make a comparison and to be fair. However, there have been times when I say, "Stop! Basta! Enough! Let's get something good to drink. Either you pick it or I will." And we will splurge every so often and treat ourselves to a good meal at an excellent restaurant, but usually not. This is business.

The other perhaps surprising thing is how often I am sick as a dog on buying trips. Once, a colleague and I were traveling south from Avignon to the fishing village of Sète, on the French Mediterranean, to visit some growers from the area whose wines I was importing. We planned to stop at Bouzigues for oysters and seafood, but halfway there I felt myself getting sick. I had a flu shot the week before, and I think I had a reaction. Doctors will tell you that this is not possible, but it's happened to me and people I know far too often to be a coincidence. I am not telling anyone *not* to get a flu shot, but for me, there can be consequences. I remember skipping dinner that night and lying on my back all night long, thrilled to have several warm blankets over me while I shivered. The next day I called my doctor and asked him what I should do. "Next time take some cipro with you," he said. Fine. There wasn't much I could do this time. I still made all my appointments.

By the way, Sète would be a great vacation spot. Located on the French Mediterranean coast, it is an attractive fishing village/port city that has a lot of natural charm, and not is not overrun by tourists. It is almost an island, with the sea out front and the Thau lagoon behind. The very large saltwater lagoon is most noted for its oyster and mussel beds.

Beautifully situated, Sète encircles one lone hill, the Mont St.-Clair, on the otherwise completely flat Languedoc coast. They have a network of canals that bring the busy port and fishing activity right into the town center. The canals define the town and energize it, as many locals use them to go shopping in their own small craft. Fishermen line the banks, and in the summer their Canal Royal is the theatre of Sète's famous waterborne jousting, something I have never seen. In Sète there is lots to do, especially if you love the ocean and fresh seafood. I am told that Sète has eight miles of some of the finest unheralded beaches of the French Mediterranean. I have never spent any time there but wish I could.

On another trip I was staying in Morey-Saint-Denis at a restaurant/hotel, Castel de Très Girard. I was so sick I couldn't even eat bread. I tried plain rice. No go. I gave my plate to one of the guys with me. Since I couldn't eat, I told them, "I am going up to my room to try and get an hour or so of rest." I left the table and started to walk across the floor to the stairway that led to my room, when all of a sudden, from behind, a dog rushed out toward me, barking like crazy. I thought it was a big dog and that I was being attacked. I whirled around instinctively, with my foot back, ready to dropkick the mutt into the next county. Just then the owner, whose dog it was, called sharply to it and it went back, tail between its legs. It wasn't that big and was not that vicious, but in my feverish state, I couldn't be sure. This all went down in seconds. I glanced over at the table where my two buddies were seated. They both had their heads down and were studiously not looking at me. "Screw 'em," I said to myself and turned to go get some rest. My next appointment was with Anne Gros, and I didn't want to be late. I wasn't.

The Passing of a Giant; The End of an Era

It's been some years since the passing of Jean Claude Vrinat, proprietor of the famous three-star Parisian restaurant Taillevent. I first met Monsieur Vrinat over twenty-five years ago. I had just started my import company, Arborway, and had a one-night stopover in Paris before bouncing off to Burgundy. This was before my daughter, Erica, moved to Paris. I called then-owner of Boston Wine Co. and longtime friend Bill Friedberg and asked him to get me a reservation at Taillevent. I told him, "I'll sit in the kitchen; I don't care." Bill was then selling, and I was buying, Taillevent Champagne. He later dropped it, and I picked it up, but that's me getting ahead of myself. Somehow, in spite of a packed Paris due to an air show, he got me a table. I showed up at the restaurant at 8:00 p.m., not yet jetlagged but beat nonetheless. As I was alone, I expected to have an enjoyable meal but not one to necessarily linger over, as I was heading out early the next day.

Right. No way. Monsieur Vrinat came over to the table to introduce himself. He was the epitome of grace. He asked what wine I would like. I said, "I could certainly find something lovely to order on your (encyclopedic) list, but I am in your hands, sir. He said, "Je vais a ma propre cave." I'll go to my personal cellar (for something). Uh oh. He came up with a half-bottle of 1982 Chevalier Montrachet-Domaine Leflaive for the white and half of 1976 Ch. Lafite Rothschild. Prices back then weren't even close to what they are today, but still. So I said to myself, "Well, you asked for it. So it'll be a special transient experience." The wine was superb, the unstuffy service beyond flawless. They made this lone diner feel at home and pampered, yet not hovered over either, all with a mischievous sense of humor.

I wish I could remember exactly what I was served, as it was fabulous. Coquilles Saint Jacques and then canard, I think. The wines were spot-on great. They complemented beautifully Taillevent's amazing cheese course. When I was given an incredible fruit-based dessert, the waiter asked if I liked it. When I said, "Yes, I loved it," he told me here's another I might like, chocolate based. Good thing I ran (jogged) back then. Let's not forget the glass of Taillevent Extra Cognac to complete my dinner.

Eventually I was ready to be poured into a taxi and go back to my hotel, not at all intoxicated but euphoric, just floating on this special experience. Moment of truth: the waiter came by and I asked, "L'addition s'il vous plaît." "Oh, you want the check, sir." he said. He came back with the check. On it was written, "Avec mes meilleures souvenirs" (With my best wishes for a good recollection) and signed Jean Claude Vrinat. I was stunned. The staff were all grinning at me, and I told them, "Your boss, il a de la classe."

Monsieur Vrinat, and I *always* called him "Monsieur Vrinat," was the most exigent person I ever dealt with, client or supplier. I did business with Jean Claude Vrinat for more than seventeen years selling his Taillevent Champagne. I had customers in nearly all fifty states before out-of-state shipping was verboten in Massachusetts. He was delightful when in the restaurant, and his warmth, personality, and intelligence infused the atmosphere, but when doing business, he was steely. He told me that he never intended to go into the restaurant business. He had gone to France's top business school, HEC Paris (l'Ecole des Hautes Etudes Commerciales), the equivalent of Wharton or MIT's Sloane School. His father, on his deathbed, made

Monsieur Vrinat promise to run the restaurant. And that was that. The seemingly block-long building housing Taillevent is a townhouse that they occupied since 1950. It was built in 1852 as a bachelor pad for Napoleon III's philandering half-brother, the Duc de Morny. It was estimated to be worth close to thirty-five million dollars or more at the time of his death. And the wine cellar: that must have been worth at least that much then, far more today, so he did OK after all.

Jean Claude Vrinat was not a large man. He was maybe five feet nine inches tall, and no athlete. But he had a magnetic personality and a charisma that made strangers feel he was a friend. Once, when he was in Boston working with us promoting his Champagne at the Four Seasons Hotel, where it was poured by the glass, my wife, Bonnie, had the nerve to invite him to our house for dinner. She said, "It's always tough to travel and eat out all the time" and "If he doesn't like this restaurant, he doesn't have to come back." She made a great meal: salad with rack of lamb, roast capon, and blueberry pie for dessert. I mulled over what wine to serve him. Sure, I could have served Burgundy or Bordeaux, but he's had lots of those. So I cleverly opted for some obscure, Rhône-like California zinfandel from a miniscule property that I was bringing in and really liked. He loved the food and appreciated being invited. He did mention how quiet Lexington was. Never said a word about the wine, so I asked. Big mistake; he *hated* it!

I know a number of you have had the good fortune of dining at Taillevent. For those who have not, you should know that the experience transcended the food. The service, setting, wines, etc. were all equally as important. Sure, there were perhaps more exciting restaurants in Paris and elsewhere, but nowhere else could one feel as if they were part of an intimate, privileged club when dining there. Just prior to Monsieur Vrinat's death the Michelin Guide, in their infinite wisdom, took a star away from Taillevent. Was it deserved? I rather doubt it, as the place was always packed. But I fear it may have contributed to Monsieur Vrinat's demise, albeit in a more subtle way than that of La Côte d'Or's owner, Bernard Loiseau, who took his own life when confronted with a lost star.

In Monsieur Vrinat's day, the staff at Taillevent was without peer, the food and the atmosphere beyond special. His wife, Sabine, and daughter, Valerie, have understandably subsequently sold off the restaurant and its holdings. I knew five years ago that Jean Claude Vrinat's passing marked the end of an era and it could never be the same. Sadly, in spite of great food and great reviews, that's true without him. I am sure his spirit, looking down from on high, also knew. Au revoir, mon ami; tu me manques.

Dining in Paris in August

In my opinion, and I am not alone in this, Paris, the "City of Lights," is the most beautiful city in the world. The dining experiences offered there are unmatched anywhere else, qualitatively and quantitatively. There are many creative new chefs who are modernizing their menus by eschewing the formal, rather stuffy, traditional French cuisine for newer, more exciting interpretations.

Six or seven years ago the French, not Japanese, restaurant Hiramatsu was recommended to us by a friend in the wine industry who said they were offering world-class, five-star dining experiences. Bonnie and I went there the next time we were in Paris, and we were blown away by the quality of the food, the presentation, and the service. It was just a tiny place but was cozy and comfortable. I remember our main course very well. It was a unique, at least to me, expression of lamb that was cut and chopped, served medium rare, and beautifully presented geometrically. Everything was just spot on. I ordered a bottle of 2001 Nuits Saint Georges Clos Lalot Domaine Lalot. It was fairly priced and delicious. The wine was, as I expected, far more Vosne in style than Nuits, with more elegance and finesse than would be expected from most Nuits Saint Georges. We left smiling.

The following year, in August, we stopped in Paris for a few days after a week's vacation in the south of France. We were excited to once again sample the cuisine at Hiramatsu. And, as they had moved to a new, more convenient if not larger location, we were curious about that as well. When we arrived, the staff seemed a bit preoccupied, not quite flustered but not clicking on all cylinders either. I asked the maître d' if they were expecting a large crowd, because even though the restaurant was only half full, everyone seemed out of breath and out of sorts. "Non, monsieur," he said, tomorrow we close the restaurant for a month and we go en vacances, on vacation. "Oh," I thought. "Uh oh." I know many establishments are closed in Paris during the month of August, but I wasn't worried—and should have been.

We ordered the same lamb dish as the year previous, and then I perused the wine list. My bottle of 2001 NSG 1er Cru Clos Lalot was still on the list, but the price had been raised by twenty euros. This was no longer a good buy. Since I decided I was not paying extra for the Nuits Saint Georges, I needed to check the list again. I spotted a bottle of 2001 Roumier Chambolle Musigny at a fair price considering where I was. I asked our waiter to send over the sommelier. He was a man in his late thirties/early forties, very tall, well over six three, cadaverously lean, with a slightly bowed back and a craggy lantern jaw. He was *not* warm and fuzzy. When traveling, I rarely if ever tell my server that I am in the wine business. I want to see what they have to say about their selections, and what they recommend. Since I hadn't had the '01 Roumier Chambolle, even though I had complete confidence in it, I asked the sommelier how it was drinking. "Ca, monsieur, c'est tres leger." That's very light, sir. "Really?" I thought to myself. "Roumier Chambolle Musigny very light?" I know Roumier adds some young-vines 1er Cru to their village wine every year, which adds depth, and 2001 was a good year for Chambolle Musigny, so that response took me aback. I wasn't looking for weight in my Burgundy choice anyway.

OK. "How is the 2003 Pommard 1er Cru Clos Blanc from Albert Grivault?" I asked. I have imported Grivault wines for many years, and while I rarely buy their Pommard, sticking to their super Meursaults, I am very familiar with the wine, so this was a test. They do not make an overly concentrated Pommard in general, but in the extra-hot 2003 vintage the wine was bigger than usual. "Ca, c'est plus leger, monsieur." It is even lighter than the Roumier. I guess I just don't know how to pick them. He then recommended an off-vintage, obscure Nuits Saint Georges from a grower that I had never heard of, at a far higher price than I wanted to spend. Bonnie was, by this time, getting fed up, so she ordered a glass of Champagne. I scanned the list again and finally, looking up at the tall fellow, ordered the Roumier after all. I now wonder at my body language.

At this point, I knew we were not going to duplicate the magic of our first visit. It soon became apparent that the entire staff could not wait to get off and out the door for the start of their long vacation. But this was, purportedly, one of the best three-star restaurants in Paris. I expected and should have received impeccable, friendly at the least, service, never mind the food. I guess my craggy-faced server was unused to Americans, or even French people, not following his advice. He went to fetch my bottle and, when he presented it to me, bent very low over the table, shoving the bottle almost in my face, with an indescribable but utterly rude, mocking leer on his visage. It was shockingly classless, completely unexpected, especially in such a setting, and unwarranted. That's right. Gratuity is included when you get the bill in France. I always leave extra for the servers, but not on this night.

To say that I was appalled would be an understatement. The food was OK, I think, if not up to the last time. I really couldn't enjoy it as much as I would have if I weren't so perturbed. The wine was, as I had hoped and expected, magnificent. After all, this was from Roumier, one of the greatest of Burgundy producers. Medium bodied, fresh, and elegant, it had a beautiful, pure bouquet that evoked black raspberries and cherries. On the palate, it had delicious spice, subtle, enticing minerality and lovely floral notes. It was quintessential Chambolle, with elegance and finesse combined with a solid tannic backbone. I had a bottle of the same 2001 Chambolle Musigny in Chablis with Jean Marc Brocard two to three years later at half the price, and it was, again, magnificent.

The experience at Hiramatsu so turned me off that, at the time, I vowed never to return. Sorry, chef. However, in looking up Hiramatsu online at Trip Advisor before writing this, I saw glowing reviews, so more than likely—one day, just maybe—I will relent and go back again. Everyone deserves a second chance. But first, I may call and make sure that the tall, craggy-faced waiter who was my nemesis that evening is no longer in their employ. Or, if I find out that he is, go there anyway just to see if he remembers me.

The lesson is, if you go to Paris in August, and you should, make sure that you reserve at a restaurant that is not closing for vacation the next day.

Arpicius

I have had my share of unusual dinner experiences in Paris over the years. One was at the acclaimed restaurant Apicius. One year, while spending a few days in Paris, Bonnie and I were hoping to try the restaurant, but reservations were impossible to come by. We vowed to reserve a table well in advance the next time to make sure we would be seated. That we did, and we finally got a reservation. We were seated at a rectangular row of tables, Bonnie facing me with her back to the wall. I was facing her and the mirror behind her. Seated next to us were a fifty-or-so-year-old mother and her son, who must have been in his early thirties. They were both smoking cigarettes when we sat down. They only time they stopped smoking was when they had food to put in their mouths. Sometimes the ashtray smoked their cigarettes for them. Nice! I could watch them in the mirror, and they knew I was not pleased. They continued to smoke, regardless.

Change tables? Not an option, as the place was, as always, completely filled. Toward the end of my meal I had had enough and called our server over. I asked her, "Do you sell cigars?" "But of course, sir. Would you like to choose?" Oh yeah, did I. I hadn't smoked a cigar in years, but this occasion warranted it. I picked a small, fat Macanudo and lit that sucker up. Guess which way I blew my smoke? Needless to say, mom and sonny were quite annoyed. I didn't care; to the contrary. What comes around goes around. Live with it. Bonnie and I had a good laugh about it later. Do I remember what I ate or drank? Not a clue.

L'Arpege

We were told that the food at Arpege, owned and operated by Alain Passard, was amazing. One summer while in Paris, I called to make a reservation and was told that if we wanted to come by for a second seating at 10:30 p.m. they would accommodate us. Really? I asked Bonnie what she thought, and she said, "Let's do it." You have to understand, we are in bed at that time when at home. But this was Paris in summer, and it was still light out after ten at night. We showed up a bit early and were given a *coupe de* Champagne and told the wait would be short. OK, all was good.

We were seated soon thereafter, and the food was fabulous: light, clean, airy, inventive, and ever so tasty. I cannot remember exactly what we ordered for dinner, mainly seafood and vegetables, but know that I loved it. I ordered a bottle of 1983 Meursault-Genevrière from Michelot-Buisson, a domaine I visited often and whose wines I knew very well. In Burgundy, 1983 was a very warm year, and I am sure that the wine had more than 13.5 percent ABV, but it wasn't hot and went great with the food. Here's where I made my mistake. After this wonderful dinner I glanced at the list of after-dinner drinks. They were offering at a very fair price some Moyet Cru Cognacs. I couldn't resist but should have. When we were leaving I was just floating on air but walking in a kind of funny, stiff-legged manner. There was a kid, maybe twelve or thirteen years of age, just outside the restaurant. Don't ask me what he was doing there that time of night. The little SOB perfectly, and with a completely straight face, mimicked the way I was walking. He looked like a mini-Prussian. All I could do is laugh and mentally tip my hat to him.

On another occasion when I was passing through Paris before going to Burgundy on business, I did what was rare for me back then.

I decided to stay over for the night and take the train for Beaune in the morning. This was well before my daughter, Erica, moved to Paris, so I was by myself. The previous experience at Arpege was so extraordinary that I decided to treat myself to lunch there. Reservations were not a problem. I had a lovely table to myself and chose their special *menu degustation* and ordered a half-bottle of 1986 Latricières Chambertin from Domaine Faiveley, not an inexpensive bottle by any means. About halfway through lunch, chef/owner Alain Passard made an appearance in the room. I watched him make the rounds of all the tables, except mine. For me, he had nothing but dirty looks. I don't have any idea what was on his mind or who he may have thought I was, but, I must admit, I was then and still am stymied. Today, I would have probably asked to have him brought to the table to ask what the deal was. Back then I was just stunned.

Helpful Hints
for Wine Lovers

Should You Cellar Wine?

Although not everyone wants or needs a wine cellar, they do come in handy. Although 99 percent of every wine on display at most shops could be brought home and enjoyed that night, there are many high-quality wines that benefit from aging, even if they may be enjoyable in their infancy. Cru Bordeaux and Burgundies as well as nebbiolo-based wines like Barolo, Barbaresco, and Gattinara, high-quality cabernet sauvignons from around the world may be considered candidates for extensive cellaring. Time in a cool, dark, vibration-free cellar would smooth out tannins while complexity is increased. But please, if you have multiple bottles of a particular wine, try one periodically to make sure they aren't going the wrong way or to see if you are happy with it now.

It's interesting and fun to observe how various wines change and develop as we enjoy them periodically over the years. I strongly suggest that people try at various times wines that were deemed worthy of aging. This is to ascertain when the balance of fruit to tannin is most pleasing, and that's all up to individual taste. I don't advocate keeping any case of wine for twelve to fifteen years untouched. There's no guarantee that, through magic or alchemy, aging any wine will make it more enjoyable. It depends on the wine, the vintage, and your preferences.

Cellaring wines to age is a good reason, but not the main reason, for a wine cellar. As much as merchants love to see their customers frequently at their shops, economically it makes good sense for them to buy wine in twelve-bottle increments to get case discounts and/or to take advantage of sales or futures offerings. Their wine would then also be readily to hand at home, which would save the time and expense of last-minute shopping. Favorite wines that are in short supply or soon to change vintage can be bought at discount and laid away for future enjoyment, saving not only money, but time as well.

What Does Having a Cellar Entail?

Over the years, I have had many people ask me to help tailor a personal cellar from scratch. That can be a lot of fun for all parties concerned. How your cellar ultimately shapes up will depend on what you'd like included and what you have allocated to spend. It doesn't have to be overly expensive, but the sky is the limit.

Thankfully, there is no hard and fast rule as to what constitutes a cellar. Some might want to have a cellar that holds four to five thousand bottles, filled with nothing but exquisite 90-plus-point-rated wines. That would be one way to go, but obviously would not be the norm. Someone in an apartment could have twenty-four assorted bottles they like, and that could conceivably be construed as having a cellar. Ideally, one should have a mix of wines that are in various stages of development: some that are young, perhaps not quite ready, and others that are ready to drink. While it's nice to have a smattering of wines from differing regions, this is your cellar and should represent your taste and cater to no one else, except perhaps your significant other. A cellar could include some favorite whites and some sparkling wine for festive occasions. But, outside of Cru Chablis, Côte d'Or whites, and chardonnays, like Mount Eden Estate, which can age and develop further complexity, it's mainly red wines that make the most sense to lay down. But it's all up to the individual as to what that may be. Why cellar California wines if you don't like them? Ditto German or Bordeaux. Or, if you prefer Italian wine or Burgundies to other regions, then that's what you should focus on.

Aside from getting enjoyment from drinking wine, many people like to just go down to check on what they've got and what might be next in line to try. That's also a big part of the fun of having a wine cellar, the tactile aspect. Some people almost never drink their cellared wines. They just go down and look at them and touch the cases. Do remember, though, you bought these to drink. Even if the rebuy or replacement price is off the charts on a wine bought for a song long ago, if you don't open and enjoy what was a great buy in the first place, it will eventually turn into vinegar and become a loss.

There's a great story, which I assume to be true, about a wine collector who lived not far from Robert Parker's Monkton, Maryland, offices. Legend has it that this fellow went to one of the *Wine Advocate* tastings, or a tasting where Robert Parker was present. After the tasting he cornered Parker and said, "I love your wine magazine, and I buy *all* the 90-point wines you recommend. I would *love* to have you come and look at my cellar. It's not far away." Parker felt trapped with no way out and said, "OK, let's do it." When they went to the proud gentleman's cellar, Parker was appalled to see case upon case of 90-point-rated but too *old* Cru Beaujolais. The man collected wine but had never tried a bottle!

When to Drink?

One of my most frequently asked wine questions is, "When is the optimum moment to drink my cellared wine?" A corollary to that, which used to apply primarily to Bordeaux bought as futures, is, "Can I afford to drink it after it has escalated so far in price since first bought?" The decision as to when to finally open a carefully cellared wine is subjective, as not everyone likes wine at the same level of development. The English are reputed to prefer their wines well aged, faded even. The French often go to the other extreme by committing vinous infanticide. Actually, Americans are reputed to best know the propitious moment. Nevertheless, I still cringe when a serious collector who just bought a case of XYZ cabernet sauvignon tells me that he is going to "cellar this for fifteen years and not touch it," when I have doubts that the wine will live half that long.

Let me again state, emphatically, don't wait too long before at least trying your cellared wines. Most wine professionals, myself included, prefer to drink their wines when they are youthfully exuberant and bursting with fruit, as opposed to when they are older and may be tired. Unless you are dealing with a great wine from a superior vintage, it's better to catch wine on its upside rather than its downside. That is, to drink the wine while it's charming and fruity and still has vibrant, youthful power. Of course, well-aged, venerable bottles from the best vintages may be the quintessential wine experience, at least intellectually. But, by contrast, old, brown, fading wines with musty aromas are beyond disappointing, especially if they were expensive, and more remains.

One of the reasons that we should be buying wine in case lots, especially as futures, is to observe their development over a period of time, and to ascertain when we might best enjoy them. I suggest that people try their cellared wines over a period of years and, when the balance of fruit to tannin pleases them, to then drink them up. Keeping any case of wine for what may be too long, untouched, and then rushing to drink it all down in less than a year is, to me, no fun at all.

The most important thing is to know your own predilections and taste and to realize that when you are happy with the way a wine tastes, that's when to drink it, no matter what you may have read or what someone may tell you.

Using Palate Memory to Buy Wine

When I first became interested in wine many years ago, I was convinced that once I tasted a particular wine I would always be able to identify it blind, even if it was mixed in with similar wines from the same vintage. Pure youthful folly (hubris)! I soon learned otherwise. Blind tastings are where you know which wines will be poured, but can't see the labels. They can be humbling experiences for even the most talented and sophisticated taster. This is especially true for double-blind tastings, where you have no clue what will be offered. Even Robert Parker, the world's most influential taster, has been red faced at blind tastings.

I am not being self-deprecating; I have had success at blind tastings. Once, at a friend's house for dinner, I correctly identified a bottle of 1961 Ch. Latour that was served blind. I had never previously tasted the wine but knew what it had to be. And as I previously wrote, I made a hit with the late, great Vosne winemaker/grower Robert Arnoux. After tasting in cask through his extensive lineup of 1er Cru and Grand Cru Burgundies, he went back to the archives and pulled out a venerable, label-less old bottle covered with dust. He asked us if we could discern the year and the appellation. When I correctly identified the wine as his 1983 Clos Vougeot, I made a friend for life.

In both of the above-related instances I pragmatically used my palate memory to identify the wines correctly. It was easier with Arnoux, as I had just tasted his Clos Vougeot and had its flavor fresh in my mind. I knew how 1983 Burgs were showing at that time, so it wasn't much of a reach to figure it out. The '61 Latour was trickier because I never tried it, but I had tasted past vintages of Ch. Latour and knew the tasting notes on this legendary wine. The wine could only have been '61 Latour, and I pegged it.

Parlor tricks aside, what is far more important than success at a blind tasting is the ability to remember what diverse wines taste like at various price points. That's so that we can mentally compare competing wines, either from the same region or at the same price point, as to quality and price. Obviously, we can't all agree on which wine is better than another, or worth more. But that doesn't change the premise that choosing the best wine for the price is how wine should be bought on any level. This is how successful professional buyers make selections for their shops or restaurants. This premise is just as true for the casual consumer as it is for professionals. The idea is to get the most value for your money.

We all have palate memory. Are you old enough to remember what a Howard Johnson's hot dog tasted like? Probably not. How about a McDonald's cheeseburger? Do you remember the taste of a favorite dish your mother made? How about the worst dish she used to make—remember that?

What's a toasted marshmallow held on a stick over a campfire taste like? Can you mentally compare a California chardonnay to chardonnay from Meursault or either of those to one from Chablis? Or California pinot noir against a Bourgogne Rouge? How about Saint Émilion against Medoc?

The only way to establish palate memory for wine is to experience as much wine as you can, at a large range of price points. The more diverse wines that you try, with an open mind, the better palate memory you will develop. But you have to remember what each wine costs, as well. Once you can do that you will be able to make better, more enlightened decisions as to what you like, what you should buy, and what you should pay.

Serve at What Temperature?

I have more than a few pet peeves regarding wine service. To head the list, I prefer to pour my own wine—or my water, for that matter. I hate it when a waitperson grabs my bottle of wine from the table and then indiscriminately begins to start to fill glasses without asking if more is desired. I will stop him or her, politely if I can. I am not happy when a white wine is served ice cold, and especially when a red wine comes too warm.

With all due respect to the many restaurateurs who do know correct procedure, it amazes me how many top-quality restaurants, *on both sides of the Atlantic*, do not have either the knowledge or the capability to store and serve fine wine at the correct temperature. How many times have you gone to a restaurant, not necessarily during the summer months, and been offered red wine that is warmer than room temperature? Where do they keep it, one wonders—under the stove? How many times have you gone to a fine restaurant and been served white wine already chilled to 35°F, with the wine person poised to stick it in an ice bucket? It is one thing if, on a summer's day, you are having an inexpensive white that may be perfectly acceptable ice cold. However, if you were having a more expensive white, from wherever, you would like to experience its inherent complexity, which would not be apparent if served too cold. Needless to say, we don't want warm white wine either.

At least with white wines you can let them warm up at the table if too cold or put them in an ice bucket filled half with ice and half with water, if not chilled enough. Red wine served too warm/hot will seem flabby, out of balance, and overly alcoholic. Sticking the bottle in an ice bucket will certainly cool it down quickly, but I have found that chilling it too quickly may shock the wine and cause it to go into a protective shell, meaning you will lose flavor and aroma. With younger reds, I may reluctantly do so at a restaurant, but at home putting the wine in the fridge for twenty to thirty minutes may be less stressful for the wine and work better, again only with younger wines. What do you do if you order a red wine by the glass and it comes warm? It happens frequently. It may seem blasphemous, but I've resorted to putting ice in the wine. Of course, you could always send it back.

Here's the deal: the easiest way to enhance wine enjoyment is to serve it at the correct temperature. High-quality reds and whites, especially Burgundies, should both be served at nearly the same temperature. In an ideal world that would be somewhere between 50–60° for red, 45–50° for white. Wines should be served less cool during winter months and cooler in the summer. I love seeing a red wine bottle beaded with sweat on a summer's day when brought up from the cellar and set on the table. It is refreshing served cool, and it gains complexity as it warms. If a white wine is brought straight from the fridge and is too cold, you only have to cradle the glass in your hands to let your body heat warm it naturally.

So try your red wines at home a little cooler than usual and your white wines a little bit less chilled. Note the flavor variations as the wine changes temperature. Of course, using "correct" wine glasses enhances the experience, and unacceptable wine glasses will detract from it.

Here's a Useful Blog Post from Tunanga Creek Winery (https://www.turangacreek.co.nz/wine-serving-temperature/)

How to serve wine at the best temperature?

Wine needs to be stored and served at the right temperature to achieve the best possible taste. Because wine is perishable, storing it at extreme temperatures will damage it.

It's safe to say that most kiwis serve their reds too warm and their whites too cold. Serving wine at the correct temperature is a bit of a challenge. The old adage "serve reds at room temperature and refrigerate whites" doesn't hold true. If you serve a wine too cool, the flavours will be disguised and if you serve wine too hot, alcohol becomes the dominant taste.

Serving a wine at the right temperature is a hard task, as you have to take into account several elements like the presence of tannins, the structure of the wine, its age, the style of the wine, etc. However, to give some advice, the table below shows suggestions on serving temperatures according to the variety you are drinking:

67 deg	Warm bath
55–58 deg	"Complex" syrah, pinot noir, cabernet sauvignon, merlot, malbec
60–62 deg	"Easy drinking" pinot noir, cabernet sauvignon, merlot, malbec
50–52 deg	Rosé wines
52–54 deg	Chardonnay, viognier, chenin blanc
48–51 deg	Riesling, sauvignon blanc, pinot gris
48–50 deg	Champagne, dessert wines
36–40 deg	Fridge temperature

The ideal serving temperature for red wines is around 57°F to 64°F, which is cooler than most homes. Therefore we recommend sometimes placing reds in the fridge for about half an hour before serving.

The ideal serving temperature for white wines is around 45°F to 55°F, which is warmer than most fridges (typically 4°C). We recommend storing whites in the fridge and removing them 1 hour before serving. Unless of course you are serving a cheap white then perhaps leave it in the fridge right up until serving to disguise the poor quality! And, if you have wine left over consider storing it in the fridge as it will last between 5 to 10 times longer.

Is It Corked? What Do I Do If It Is?

Most of us in the wine business occasionally lose sight of the fact that the vast bulk of our customers do not share our passion for wine. We often assume that they know more about wine and care far more about it than they actually do. That's because we care so much. Undoubtedly, most patrons even at a relatively good restaurant wouldn't have a clue what I meant if I declared, "This wine is corked." Hopefully the servers would.

There's a very good reason why you are asked to taste a sample before accepting a wine when dining out. And it's not to see if you are happy with your choice. A small percentage of wines are tainted by bad corks. The wine person or waiter at a restaurant traditionally pours the guest who did the ordering, or is designated to taste, a small amount of wine to be tried to make sure it's "good." Usually it is not nearly enough to discern anything; most may as well use an eyedropper. Feel free to ask for more to be poured so you have enough to swirl and sample.

I shudder to think of the innumerable corked bottles that are accepted and drunk in spite of their flaws because those who chose them, at home or dining out, thought they just didn't like the wine, or worse, don't like wine at all.

Here's the deal: while some wines are so blatantly corked that no way would you accept or drink them, the cork taint in some wines is so subtle as to be almost undetectable … initially. I know that on more than one occasion, both here and in Europe, I have tasted and accepted my wine selection only to go back to it shortly after it had been poured and only then, on next sip, realize that it was corked. *The thing about corked wines is that they never get uncorked.* Air only exacerbates the cork taste, which features musty, off-putting aromas, some say like old sweatsocks or a dirty-clothes hamper. Or it may smell like a wet basement after flooding. Not nice. On the palate, if you get that far, it will taste like it smells maybe out of balance, sharp, and lacking fruit. I have had a couple of instances where a (subtly) corked wine was so rich and brimming with fruit that I drank at least some of it before it really got bad; however, I don't recommend that for others. One positive is that corked wines will not make you sick.

So what should you do if you have already accepted a wine (at a restaurant) and subsequently find it corked? What I've done is to call the waiter or person in charge over and calmly explain that I believe that the wine is corked and I ask them to please try it. I offer to pay if they disagree with my assessment, but I refuse to drink that wine and choose another bottle of about the same price to replace it, regardless. I have never had to pay. There are some restaurateurs who refuse to acknowledge that they could possibly sell a corked wine, but they are, thankfully, rare and usually will make the swap anyway.

Here's an exception. An English expatriate courtier based in Avignon told me this story. The owner of an English wholesale wine-distribution company to whom he sold F. E. Trimbach Alsace wines was visiting him in France. They went to a restaurant, where they had listed Trimbach's Riesling Cuvée Frédéric Émile. They ordered a bottle and upon tasting realized that it was corked. They asked the supercilious waiter to taste it to verify the condition of the wine. He refused. Can you imagine? He refused to even try the wine! Of course, being English gentlemen they were very polite, but they refused to drink that bottle and ordered another bottle of Frédéric Émile that was fine. After the meal, the English importer informed their haughty, not pleasant, arrogant waiter who he was and that he had been selling Trimbach wines for over thirty-five years. The Englishman never raised his voice, but he cut this waiter to pieces verbally, and he didn't even know he was bleeding.

Happily, the percentage of corked wines is diminishing as use of alternative closures, such as screw caps and synthetic and composite corks, has increased dramatically in recent years. With young, inexpensive reds and whites, especially, screw caps work well. But I wouldn't want 1er Cru Burgundies, Classified Bordeaux, or Cru Barolo to use them, because while they are functional they are certainly not romantic. Also, conscientious, quality-oriented producers, with wines at various price points, are using better-quality corks to protect what they worked so hard to produce. That doesn't mean you will never serve or be served a flawed bottle. You should be aware that they exist and what to do if you get one.

If ever you get a bad or corked wine at retail, cork it up and bring it back. Honorable merchants—and most are—will replace it with the same or a comparable wine. But don't wait, and *do not* empty the bottle. They only get credit from their distributor on mostly full bottles, never empties.

None of us is exempt from corked wines. Some years back, my wife, Bonnie, and I were celebrating our anniversary at a fine, small Vermont inn. They had some nice wines listed but, as this was a special anniversary, I asked if I could take my own carefully hoarded bottle of 1996 Romanée-Saint-Vivant. I joked with the wine steward that this should be a killer bottle, unless it was corked. You guessed it. I should have kept my mouth shut. It was corked, not blatantly, but enough to be virtually undrinkable, although I tried. We went to plan B and chose from their list.

No wine, regardless of pedigree, is immune to cork taint, even if the producer buys the highest-quality corks. I've been to tastings at Domaine de la Romanée Conti, Domaine Leflaive, Ch. Cos d'Estournel, and Ch. Ducru Beaucaillou where a corked bottle was in evidence. At group tastings it's funny to observe the expressions on various tasters' faces as they struggle to comprehend that a bottle of high repute might have a problem. Most deny the fact outright or blame themselves for not understanding the wine. "This wine couldn't possibly be 'bad,' could it?" And I'm talking about professionals here.

While in Puligny years back, just back from Alsace, Olivier Leflaive stopped me one early evening on the street in front of my hotel. He invited me to a vertical tasting of Domaine Leflaive Chevalier Montrachet with himself and Anne-Claude Leflaive at Domaine Leflaive, just up the street from where I was staying. Of course I said yes. Clive Coats was invited, as were five or six of the top area sommeliers. It was a memorable, extensive, totally incredible tasting, with some of those great wines served in magnums and some that were the last bottles of the vintage at the domaine. Well, when the 1982 Chevalier was served, it was corked—not badly, but it was obvious to me. Do you think I opened my mouth to alert Olivier or Anne-Claude? No way, and neither did any of the sommeliers, some if not all of whom had to know. But, bless him, larger-than-life Clive Coates bellowed out, "Hey, this wine is corked!" 'Ce vin la, c'est bouchonné!" he shouted. A very funny and extraordinary experience.

By the way, don't be confused if you see mold on the top on the cork when you strip the foil. That does not mean that the wine is going to be bad or corked. The *only* way to tell is to pop the cork. A bottle is not corked just because it has bits of cork in it, probably caused by the waiter pushing the corkscrew all the way through the cork, with pieces falling into the wine. You cannot tell if a wine is corked by smelling the cork, although it might give you a hint. Many perfectly fine wines have been poured from bottles with funky-smelling corks, and vice versa.

To Decant or Not?

Whether to decant wine or not before serving is a very personal and often controversial topic. While there are no hard-and-fast rules about decanting, some truisms apply. First and foremost, one should not be dogmatic about it, as not all wines will benefit from being decanted, and others may just get pushed off a cliff. Current-vintage wines like pinot grigio, Beaujolais, Sancerre, etc. are not candidates. They have no need to be decanted and would not change positively if they were. There are some restaurants, here and abroad, that somehow feel compelled to decant everything they serve, without discussion. I politely ask them to stop before they start and allow me to taste. I may ultimately agree, but I need to be consulted first and then convinced. Some people, similarly, decant everything, assuming that by doing so the taste and texture of the wine will improve. Not always, however, and sometimes to the contrary.

Many years ago, by losing a treasured last bottle of '59 Bordeaux, I learned a hard lesson: older wine can be ruined by extensive decanting. I have been conservative ever since. Older bottles of great wine may well need to be decanted, as sediment can build up, add a negative flavor to the wine, and mar its texture. That's why I suggest standing bottles up for a minimum of day or two, so the built-up sediment coating the sides of the bottle can drop down and settle. Standing them for a week would even be better, then decant and serve immediately. It's better to let the wine come up in your glass, rather than having it possibly go over.

Of course, it all depends on which older wine. I remember fondly that we were invited to a friend's house for dinner and, when we arrived, he had already opened and decanted a 1959 Ch. Mouton Rothschild. This had to be twenty or so years ago, so the wine was around forty years of age. I had never had this vintage of Mouton but knew its reputation for being a *big* wine. It had been opened for more than an hour when I asked my friend, "Aren't you afraid that it might go over?" He said, "OK, fine. Let's just have it now rather than later." Some aperitif wine! It was fabulous, big as houses, and would have more than likely been great the next day. But that is an anomaly. It was Mouton Rothschild, once called famously "a Churchill of a wine"! I'm not sure that today even First Growth Bordeaux could match the power of that '59 Mouton.

I would hardly ever consider decanting Burgundy, unless I was dealing with a venerable old bottle that had a lot of sediment built up, and then only after it had been standing for quite a while. Pinot noir grapes are thinner skinned than cabernet sauvignon or merlot grapes, so Burgundies are usually not overly tannic. There are some exceptions (Grands Crus), but they are in the minority. I must add, although it may seem counterintuitive, young white Burgundy Crus, like Corton Charlemagne, or Mount Eden Estate Chardonnay, can benefit from being decanted. I was initially shocked when I saw Burgundian vignerons doing this, but it did improve the drinkability of the wine.

Speaking of Burgundy, more than twenty years ago I became friendly with François Faiveley. During the 1988 harvest he invited me to stay in the vacant condo apartment that used to belong to his aunt. It was adjacent to his apartment in Nuits Saint Georges. While I was there, he was hosting a tasting and luncheon for Robert Parker, and I was invited. This was, of course, well before their famous estrangement.

Someone must have given François or his dad a bottle of 1919 Ch. Margaux. It's pretty much a given that Burgundians know little and care less about Bordeaux, and François was no exception. He passed the bottle to me and asked me to uncork and decant it. Gulp! The cork was all covered with muck, but it was removed with no problem. Taking no chances, I gently and carefully decanted the wine, leaving a good quarter of it, mostly dark sludge sediment, in the bottle. When the wine was finally poured out, I took a sniff, then a taste and, very ingenuously if not intelligently, turned to Christophe, the Faiveley export manager, and reflexively said, "Il est mort." The wine is dead. He looked at me, horrified, and I shut up.

It is much more practical and makes far more sense to decant young, tannic red wines to soften them up and improve their taste and texture. Older wines may be more delicate or fragile and are more vulnerable to air. Prime candidates for decanting are: Bordeaux; certain California cabernet sauvignons; super Tuscan reds; southern and, especially, northern Rhône wines; and many Italian reds, especially Barolo, Barbaresco, and Gattinara from the Piedmont.

Once you have decided to decant, the question is for how long. I reiterate: don't be dogmatic. Once you uncork a wine that you expect to decant, try it first, even if you've decanted and served it before. Don't just blithely pour without knowing how *this* particular bottle is showing now. Bottles vary in their case. There is no guarantee that another bottle of the same wine from the same case will be a duplicate of the one served on another occasion. With an older wine, it may well show differently. If in doubt as to whether to decant or not, don't. Just wait. Try your wine again in thirty minutes or so after opening. If it's still showing overly tannic, then decant. I sometimes will open a bottle and leave it for an hour or more and then decant just before dinner is served.

I find that Piedmont-area wines are the ones that I decant most often. They are generally pretty much bulletproof, and even a ten-year-old Barolo, especially if it's a Cru, can generally stand three hours of air, softening and improving. I did a vertical tasting at the home of one of my friends with sixteen to eighteen of us in attendance. Bottles of 2004, 2005, 2006, 2008, and 2009 Barolo Giachini from Giuliano Corino were served along with 2004 Barolo Arborina, also from Corino. Later we compared 2006 Azelia Barolo Margheria with Luigi Pira's 2006 Margheria. We gave them all an hour or two of air, no decanting, and then we tried them over more than three hours. The wines showed beautifully from go, but it was a revelation how they changed and developed further as the evening progressed. Layer upon layer of iridescent flavors cascaded on our palates kaleidoscopically. Would we have missed that development if they had been decanted for three to four hours in advance? Undoubtedly, so that is why no rules apply here.

Wine Scores—Are They Useful?

As a wine professional I read multiple wine-oriented periodicals. Domestically, Robert Parker's *Wine Advocate*; Antonio Galloni's *Vinous*, which now has incorporated Stephen Tanzer's *International Wine Journal*; Allen Meadow's *The Burghound*; and *Wine Spectator* all come readily to mind. Internationally, the *Guide Hachette Vins*, *Revue de Vins de France*, and *Gambero Rosso* are also educational. I used to follow Clive Coates's *Vine*, especially for his Burgundy writeups, but he stopped writing it some years ago.

I like to cross-check opinions from various sources to see if there is or is not a consensus about different vintages and individual wines. Coates was entertaining as an "anti-Parker," disagreeing not only with many of his wine assessments but his method of grading as well. In scanning some older issues of Coates's *Vine* I came across an interesting article he had written in February 2003 concerning numerical marking. He called the article "Marking Within Context—An Explanation." It's important to know that Coates had no intention of ever putting numerical scores on wines he was reviewing, as he felt that words alone should be used to describe wine, not numbers. However, reader demand forced him to put numerical ratings on his words. Utilizing a 20-point system, not the more typical 100 points of Parker and the *Spectator*, he would offer the following: a wine called "excellent-Grand Vin" was equal to 20 out of 20 points. "Very fine indeed" was 19.5 points. A wine labeled "very good indeed" was equal to 17 points; one called "good" was a 15-pointer, etc.

Here's how I see it: Regardless of which rating system one uses, there are natural inequities between different wines, even those with the same numerical score. Example: What do these three wines at different price points, different regions, and different vintages have in common? 2015 Côtes du Rhône Villages ($15.99 a bottle), 2010 Ch. Fombrauge-Saint Emilion ($59.99 a bottle), and 2013 Gaja Ca'Marcanda ($125 a bottle). All three are Parker rated at 90 points. Other than the fact they are all red wines, the answer is, "nothing but the score."

So what do the numbers really mean? Coates says that marking within context (of the vintage and region) is the only logical way. Therefore an 89-point-rated Beaujolais and an 89-point-rated Grand Cru Classé Bordeaux, both with the same score, are not equal. The Beaujolais can be enjoyed immediately for a few years tops; the Bordeaux may need up to a decade to become approachable. Similarly, but more subtly, a 91-point-rated 2011 Vosne Romanée Suchots from Jadot would probably not be equal in quality to a 91-point-rated Jadot Vosne Romanée Suchot from either 2012 or 2010. Both 2012 and 2010 were stronger vintages than 2011, so 91 points for them carries more weight than 91 points from the 2011 vintage. The numerical rating is the same for both because they were rated within the context of their own vintage. Jadot's 2011 Suchot excelled against the "competition" that existed within the context of the 2011 vintage only—Ditto Jadot's Suchot from 2012 and 2010. This is not an easy point to get across.

Two friends in discussing the merits of two pizzerias, one local, the other the next town over, may argue about which one offers better food or more value. These are more or less in the same context. But if they were comparing a local Italian restaurant with a fancier, more expensive spot in Boston that had more ambiance but not necessarily much better food, that's not quite the same but is still within the same context. However, the local Italian restaurant should not be compared to a top Boston restaurant like Mistral, Nine Park, Deuxave, or the now closed Hamersley's. That would be unfair. Value judgments need to be made within their context. We do the same with wine by *not* comparing a southern French chardonnay to a Puligny-Montrachet. It's not a fair comparison; it's out of context.

What about the context of price points? Shouldn't that figure into the ratings mix? How about longevity? Michel Rolland's Clos de la Siete Chilean red was awarded 92 Parker points. The totally delicious 2009 Chambolle Musigny Villages from Hudelot-Noëllat was rated 89 from hard-marking Allen Meadows, the Burghound.com.

One retails for twenty dollars, the other for eighty dollars. Is Clos de la Siete a "better" wine and a better value? Which would you prefer to drink if offered both even up, and with what? While both are good in their context, they don't compete with each other, as they are in different categories (contexts) of wine and moreover were judged by different people. Furthermore, although I would drink it, I still wouldn't recommend the elegant Chambolle to go with pot roast or grilled sausages, but the more rustic Clos de la Siete or a Côtes du Rhône would be better than fine.

Coates claims that all wine journalists, whether they realize it or not, assess wines within context. He writes, "It is implicit in the words they use, if not consistently the marks. 'This is a brilliant wine given an overall poor vintage,' go the comments. 'This is a major disappointment for such a normally overachieving property.' And so on. The only marking system which can reflect this is one marking within a context."

Understandably, judging wine is subjective and highly personal, whether you are a professional or just a weekend imbiber. Have you ever gone to a formal wine tasting where you listen to comments from others tasting the same wine as you, but what they are saying doesn't compute? That's normal. People, thankfully, have different palates and different preferences. That's why even so-called wine professionals have differing views of the same wines and why I like to compare their notes to my perceptions.

I hope this doesn't confuse people. I am just making the point that numerical scores often are perplexing and shouldn't be taken as gospel. Take Parker, for example. He is proud of being the most rapid taster on the planet, and I've been with him at tastings and believe it may be true. But if he tastes and rates numerically fifty wines in an hour, would the first wine receive the same score if it were retasted as the fifty-first? Would another bottle of the same wine from a different case receive the same score if served at dinner that night? Or tasted in a different context next week?

So, yes, the scores given to wines by respected wine journalists are useful to *amateurs du vin* and professionals alike. It's wise to know the predilections of the wine writers in the various periodicals and the context in which the wines are being judged. But it's more important to know your own predilections. Who cares what they like if you don't agree. And the converse is true.

How to Read European Wine Labels. How Do We Know What Grapes Were Used?

Choosing an imported wine can be perplexing for many wine lovers. The majority of European wines, excepting Germany and Alsace, do not indicate what grape varieties are included. Whereas, by contrast, California, Oregon, Australia, New Zealand, and South African make things easier for consumers, as they invariably have the grape varieties listed on the label.

European wine labels may include a great deal of information, but often not the grape variety. Most are labeled generically with the name of the region, village, or vineyard site where they were produced: Bourgogne Blanc or Bourgogne Rouge, Pouilly-Fuissé, Pauillac, Barolo, Bordeaux, Taurasi, Brunello di Montalcino, Morellino di Scansano, Châteauneuf du Pape, etc. are all just examples of wines whose labels give no information as to the grape varieties included. And, if blended, they usually do not indicate what grapes were used and in what proportion. We, the wine-consuming public, are expected to at least know what grapes each wine-producing region uses, which often is a faulty assumption.

Obviously, European winemakers are not trying to confuse us by excluding information about the grape varieties of their wines on their bottles. It's just that this is how their wines have been labeled since forever. Allow me to (try to) clarify: there are two ways to discern the information found labeled on a bottle of wine:

One way is varietally, and the other is generically.

1) **Varietal**. A wine may be labeled by the grape "variety" from which it was made: pinot noir, chardonnay, cabernet sauvi-

gnon, merlot, nebbiolo, dolcetto, barbera, sauvignon blanc, syrah, viognier, marsanne, rousanne, vermentino, pinot grigio, etc.

2) **Generic refers to the place name** from whence the wine comes: Burgundy, Bordeaux, Gattinara, Chianti, Langhe, Barolo, Languedoc, Chinon, etc. Varietals are self-explanatory, so let me give you some simple, basic examples of some major generic wines.

France: Nearly 100 percent of red Burgundies are made from 100 percent pinot noir grapes. Beaujolais is made 100 percent from gamay. Nearly 100 percent of white Burgundies are made exclusively from chardonnay grapes. (If you would like to know the not-worth-thinking-about exceptions, they are aligote, sauvignon de Saint Bris, and a tiny amount of pinot blanc from Nuits Saint Georges.) Sancerre and Pouilly-Fumé are 100 percent sauvignon blanc. Vouvray is 100 percent chenin blanc. Savennières and Quart de Chaume are also made from 100 percent chenin blanc grapes. Chinon Rouge is 100 percent cabernet franc. Muscadet, produced in the Loire near Nante, is made from melon de bougogne grapes.

Red Bordeaux are made up of a blending of cabernet sauvignon, merlot, cabernet franc, and petit verdot. Each château has its own blend. White Bordeaux are blends of sauvignon blanc and sémillon. Southern Rhône, including Châteauneuf-du Pape, Gigondas, and Vacqueyras and most other southern French wines, are blends mostly of syrah, grenache, mourvedre, carignon, and cinsault. Hermitage and Côte-Rôtie (some Côte-Rôtie producers add a trace of viognier) are 100 percent syrah, as is red Crozes Hermitage. Condrieu is made from 100 percent viognier grapes.

Italy: Piedmont wines such as Barolo, Gattinara, Ghemme and Barbaresco are produced from 100 percent nebbiolo grapes. Wines from Valtellina, from Lombardy, are 100 percent nebbiolo as well. Chiantis are made up of blends of sangiovese and canaiolo. Super Tuscans, such as Tignanello, Sassacaia, Solaia, etc. are blends of sangiovese and cabernet sauvignon or merlot. The super Tuscan Ornellaia is 55 percent–65 percent cabernet sauvignon, 20 percent–25 percent merlot, plus smatterings of cabernet franc and petit verdot.

Other Tuscan wines, such as Brunello di Montalcino and Vino Nobile di Montepulciano, are made up of various clonal varieties of sangiovese. However, Montepulciano d'Abruzzo is made from the grape variety of that exact same name—Montepulciano. And barbera, dolcetto, falanghina, erbaluce, and sangiovese are grape varieties, not places. Gavi is a region in the Piedmont that makes nice dry white wine. Vernaccia is a grape variety noted for being grown in vineyards outside of San Gimignano.

That's far enough; you get the idea. I'm not going get into the different grape varieties found in Spanish or Portuguese wines. And Italian wines from Sicily, Puglia, and Calabria are made with any number of relatively obscure grape varieties. I see no need to delve into those at this time. I just wanted to give some guidelines to those of you who may not have been aware of the varietal/generic distinction of many of our favorite wines so that you can buy better, with more confidence, and enjoy wine more.

What Is Organic Wine?
Misconceptions Abound

Many enlightened consumers make an effort to buy organic products, wine included. To be certified 100 percent organic today, the USDA requires that a wine must be made from organically grown grapes *without* any sulfites used in any way. The vast majority of wines that previously were allowed to be labeled simply as "organic" had minimal amounts of sulfites used in their production to protect them from oxygen and bacteria. These wines must now be labeled "wines made with organic grapes" or "produced from organically grown grapes." Of course, wines produced with "Organically Grown Grapes" means that no pesticides, insecticides, or chemical fertilizers are used. Only natural fertilizers are applied.

Many people assume, incorrectly, that a wine with "organically grown grapes" on its label is made without sulfites. Sulfur dioxide is used in the winemaking process, although in far smaller amounts than is the case with nonorganics. Sulfur dioxide is not a bad thing; to the contrary, wineries and their equipment must be kept pristine. SO_2 is the sanitizing agent in the cellar used to clean the barrels and equipment. It serves as an antibacterial and antioxidant, protecting wine from spoilage.

Organic practice in the vineyard is one thing, but biodynamic agriculture is something else again. It was first introduced by Rudolph Steiner, an Austrian scholar and spiritualist, who is reputed to have advocated a new method of holistic farming that went far beyond organic. He aligned vineyard work with forces of nature, the rhythms of the moon, and the position of the stars.

Many of the best wineries in the world now exclusively employ biodynamic practices, with an ever-increasing number joining the ranks each year. To name a few: Domaine de la Romanée Conte, Maison Remoissenet, Domaine Joseph Drouhin, and Domaine Leflaive in Burgundy; Coulée de Serrant in the Loire; Jean Marc Brocard and Long Depaquit in Chablis; Chapoutier in the Rhône; and Marco Parusso in the Piedmont. There are many other winemakers who have proven the efficacy of this method to improve and preserve their land and make better wine. Many have now ditched their John Deere plows to return to plowhorses for field work. Most of those who do practice biodynamic viticulture, or organic viticulture, don't bother to apply for label certification. The hoops that have to be jumped through are just too high. The list of those who fall into this category is endless. The Benziger Family Winery in California is a prime example.

Nicolas Joly, owner of the fabulous Loire estate Coulée de Serrant, is very much into biodynamic viticulture. His business cards reportedly read "Nature Assistant and Not Winemaker." Joly's book, *Wine from Sky to Earth: Growing and Appreciating Biodynamic Wine*, was first published in 1999 and has been translated into nine languages. The Benzigers reportedly used this book as a guide to bring Joly's

French concept of biodynamics to their Sonoma estate. Joly, from all reports, is a fascinating man. He was a highly successful, therefore wealthy, investment/banker with an MBA from Columbia. Legend has it that when his dad died and his mother needed help at the farm, he quit his lucrative job and enthusiastically went back to work the soil. Initially he used traditional methods in the fields: herbicides, chemical fertilizers, insecticides, etc.

Quoting from Robert V. Camuro's interesting book, *Cork Screwed,* which I highly recommend, Joly says, "After two years I went into the vineyard and saw that I had destroyed something. The color of the soil had completely changed. It became paler and harder. The insects, the lady bugs, were no longer there." Up until then Joly had little regard for ecologists. "To me ecologists were city people who knew nothing about nature," he is quoted as having said. Then he was given Steiner's book. Quoting Camuto, "He took one hectare (2 ½ acres) and stopped using chemicals, turned the soil with horse and plow, used only organic soil preparations and applied healing herbs to the plants and soil, all timed to the celestial calendar." Within a year the experiment was a success. He had better-quality grapes due to deeper roots, which extract more nutrients from the soil, which resulted in far better wine. By 1984 the entire vineyard was operating biodynamically. His Coulée de Serrant, 100 percent chenin blanc, is brilliant and sought the world over despite its expense.

Joly sites four tragedies of modern winemaking (*quatres drames*):

- The first tragedy is use of herbicides. Plants can't live without microorganisms, and herbicides kill them.

- The second tragedy is use of chemical fertilizers to make up for the lack of food in the soil due to use of herbicides.

- The third tragedy are systematic treatments that penetrate into the plant sap, theoretically to compensate for the overfertilizing. Joly says, in Camuto's book, "Sap is the plant's telephone for talking to the sun. If you poison the sap, you cut off the plant's ability to communicate with the sun and you poison the plant's capacity to control the taste, smell and color of the fruit. *Modern agriculture guarantees a big harvest but destroys the original taste of the fruit."*

- Joly's fourth tragedy is technology. Meaning the technological tricks employed by some "winemakers" to compensate for tasteless fruit by adding flavor-enhancing yeasts. This is far more common in bulk wines, and others, than one would think. I am not making a list, but if I did, you might be surprised by some of the well-known names. Go back and read the last sentence of the last paragraph. There are a lot of very popular wines that I would not recommend; "to the contrary."

The fact is, there are a myriad of affordable, interesting wines out there that have been carefully made with respect shown to nature and the environment, as well as to you and me.

Lunar Cycles and Wine

A number of highly intelligent people, winemakers and wine merchants alike, now believe that lunar cycles can influence wine. Ch. Romanin in Baux en Provence, for example, has been cultivating their vineyards using biodynamic viticulture for years. Their all-natural method is based on lunar cycles that they believe affect the quality of their plants. Julien Brocard uses the same method in his wonderful Chablis vineyard, La Boissoneuse. Dominique Lafon and Domaine Sauzet are also certified biodynamic. Ever-increasing numbers of enlightened, pragmatic growers around the world are doing likewise, as they are convinced that biodynamic viticulture produces better wine while protecting the long-term health of the soil.

It's not just grape growing that is affected by the moon; wine tastings may be as well. A German great-grandmother, Maria Thun, has had a very significant influence on the British wine industry. Her theory, first stated in a book published in the '50s, is that wine is a living organism that responds to the moon's rhythms, as do, apparently, some people. She created a calendar that categorizes days as "fruit," "flower," "leaf," or "root," according to the positions of the moon and stars. Wine supposedly tastes best on fruit days and flower days, with leaf and then root days less good.

British mega supermarkets Tesco and Marks & Spencer support her philosophy and only invite critics or buyers to taste wine on fruit or flower days. Quoting Jo Aherne conducting a tasting at Marks & Spencer, "I was skeptical at first, but then had a eureka moment. Our wines showed beautifully at a press tasting one day and far less well the next. We couldn't understand it. The wines were all favorites of ours and the bottles were all from the same case. Someone checked the calendar and we found that the first day had been a fruit day, when the wines were expressive, exuberant and aromatic, and the second a root day, when they were closed, tannic and earthy. Further rather unscientific tests have confirmed our view."

Needless to say, many are skeptical about this theory. However, as anyone who tastes wine for a living knows, the same wine can and often does taste differently on different days. Sure, beyond Thun's lunar calendar there are many reasons why, but the Thun theory may offer one. I'm certainly no scientist and am by nature a skeptic, but I must admit, during the periodic tastings I hold for my staff, I have most certainly noted some surprises. On occasion, wines that absolutely should have shown beautifully have lacked fruit, clarity, and varietal typicity. Last year, samples of new vintages from an always excellent, small California producer were received in pristine condition and were well rested before we tried them. We were very disappointed and, after this tasting, my staff wanted to discontinue the brand. As I very much like this grower and his wife, who have put me up and fed me (well) at their home, I said, "Not so fast; it must have been a root day."

Knowing how proud and serious these people are, I reluctantly emailed them the results. I did add the disclaimer that this must have been a root day, and would they please send another set of wines. They were stunned and confused but sent us a new set to try. They were vindicated at the next tasting, as the wines showed the usual excellent quality. We placed an order.

So was it a root day first go-round? Was the wine negatively affected by travel? Or could it have been a "fruit day" when it tasted so good the second time? No clue. But, guess what—I wouldn't bet against the German grandma.

The Use of Wood in Making Wine

The use of new oak barrels for aging wine is prevalent in most parts of the world. It's no longer just Bordeaux and Burgundy that employ small oak casks, but now the Piedmont, Tuscany, California, Australia, and Spain, etc. invest in them as well. Let's be clear: I am not against using wood for wines that can handle it. Undoubtedly, judicious use of wood for wines that have sufficient material or substance can add a great deal to the flavor of the wine. It can round out any rough edges while adding structure and definition. Certain wines crave new wood and absorb it beautifully. First Growth Bordeaux and Grand Cru Burgundies, both red and white, require aging in at least some, up to 100 percent, new oak barrels in good vintages. Like a beautiful painting, these wines deserve to have a beautiful "frame." This is also true of many high-quality California cabs or chardonnays, which are enhanced by its use. Several modern Barolo winemakers, such as Sandrone, Voerzio, Corino, and Azelia age at least some of their wine in new oak barrels. Barbera, in good years, sops it up like a sponge.

New wood barrels are very expensive. Quality Allier or Limousine barrels that hold approximately three hundred bottles can cost over $1,000 each. Why waste these barrels on wine not strong enough to support them? The use of new wood, integrated in wines able to support it, can add to our wine-drinking pleasure. However, there are many wines, like Sancerre, nonpremier cru Chablis, Beaujolais, dry Italian whites, certain Tuscan wines, etc. that are better off without it and are spoiled by its use.

Obviously, not all vintages are equal; some produce more powerful wines than others. If a winemaker blindly uses the same amount of new wood each year regardless of the quality of the vintage, in some years the wines may be overwhelmed by it, and in others not have enough. Domaine Laurent, in the past, was reputed to have employed what they call "200 percent new wood." Regardless of vintage, they used to age their Burgundies in 100 percent new wood and after some months transfer the wine to virgin barrels. Some years their wines were great, other years all one could taste is the wood. They have since changed their methods and no longer do that.

Tasting once with renowned, iconoclastic Burgundy producer Jean-Marie Guffens, he once sardonically said about a wine we were trying, "It's not over wooded, it's under wined." I've always loved that and wished that I had said it.

The French liken the use of new wood to their word *maquillage*, or make-up. A beautiful woman uses just a small amount of cosmetics to enhance her natural charm. Too much would be counterproductive and "mask" her beauty. To continue the analogy, but not meaning to be sexist: a less fortunate, less attractive person might use excessive amounts of cosmetics, to no avail. Or, rather, a good wine can be ruined by too much wood, while a mediocre wine will not be saved, no matter the amount.

Barrel Making

Barrel making is an art, and the process is passed down from generation to generation. The five most important French forests for barrel production are Allier, Limousin, Nevers, Tronçais, and Vosges. They each have wood with distinctive characteristics of wood grain as well as oak flavors.

The use of wood barrels, new or old, is a lot like using spice in cooking. This is especially true now, when there are different flavors of barrels, with some from Allier, some from Limousine, even some from Pennsylvania. There are barrels with differing degrees of toast, ordered by winemakers to their specifications. Wood should be used to add flavor or accentuate. While everyone has a different idea as to how to cook, no one would consciously put an overabundance of salt, pepper, or any other spice into something they were cooking when just a small amount would enhance rather than overwhelm.

Blind Tastings; Why Bother?

Some people attach negative connotations to blind tastings, apparently thinking that those who engage in them must be pompous or pretentious. Of course, there are wine-tasting groups at various levels, blind or otherwise. If there is a theme to the tasting and you can increase your wine knowledge, having fun doing it, then go for it.

There will always be people who think blind tastings are simply a way for "wine geeks" to show off; however, that is *not* why blind tastings are held. It is possible that some people may try to use blind tastings as a way to show off, but more than likely, they are going to end up looking like fools. In any case, that is not why wine professionals, or others serious about wine, have blind tastings. For those with no ego problems and a willingness to learn, blind tastings can be very educational, if not occasionally humbling. The fact is, you have to have a lot of nerve and self-confidence to taste wine blind with a group, as you have an excellent chance of getting egg on your face; I don't care who you are, Bob Parker included.

When you sample and taste as many wines as do most wine professionals, palates can become biased, positively and negatively, toward certain producers, regions, styles, or varietals. And labels can deceive. Tasting blind keeps wine buyers impartial and focused on what is in the glass, *not* on the tell-all label. Believe me, any of us can get conned by a label. It has happened to me more than once. How could that wine be corked? It's Ducru Beaucaillou! In a blind tasting, especially if it is double blind, where you have no idea—not one clue—about what you will be tasting, you must focus only on what is in the glass. Do you like it? Where is it from? What's the grape variety or varieties? What should it sell for? One can't look at anything but the quality and potential price. If you like it, what would you pay for it, and will it sell? If it is less expensive than you might have expected, then great. Of course, if you do not like the wine, the price matters not at all.

My colleague Alex Bluhm came up with this:

"Here's an abstract music-related analogy that supports blind tastings: Many songwriters do not like to discuss their personal meaning or motivation behind songs they write because once the song is released, it can mean anything to anyone. It may be sad to one person and incredibly uplifting to someone else. The songwriter does not want his personal interpretation to turn someone else off to his song. Without context, all you know is whether you like it or not. It's a good way to tell whether a song moves you of its own volition.

But there are some key wine people who write blind tastings off entirely. Kermit Lynch in his book, *Adventures on the Wine Route*, states, "Blind Tasting is to wine drinking what strip poker is to love." Perhaps Kermit simply meant that blind tastings are embarrassing and ultimately humbling? More likely, however, what Kermit meant when he compared blind tasting to strip poker is that blind tasting really has nothing to do with *drinking wine* as such. Kermit believes that in order to enjoy drinking wine, you should know everything about how the wine was made: The producer, the tradition, the vineyard, the ageing, vinification methods, etc. I think that may be all well and good, but is completely unnecessary.

Here's a similar music-related comparison for Kermit's side of the argument: Was Eric Clapton's "Tears in Heaven" as moving when you didn't know the story behind it? Knowing the circumstances of the song, and what the musician put into that song, can't help but change how you feel about it.

When I'm just drinking wine (for pleasure), I want to

know as much as possible (about it) so I can have an understanding of what went into this product. In my opinion, blind tastings are different. They can be a valuable tool in assessing wines impartially because often you'll be surprised at what you find that you like, what you actually write off, and what you thought would happen (in the tasting). One thing is for sure though, like strip poker, blind tastings are fun!"

Again this was written by Alex Bluhm, when twenty-seven years old. God love him.

Some Additional Interesting Personages

I have written about many of the people I have encountered during my wine journey through life. All of them were included because they had strong, obviously memorable personalities and high intellect. However, I would be remiss if I didn't include four others. I never met Pauline de Rothschild but feel compelled to include her, as her passing reminded me of an unforgettable meeting forty years ago with her father, Baron Philippe de Rothschild.

Over the years, I have had many wonderful employees and some far less than wonderful, if truth is to be told. The good outnumber the bad by a lot, thank goodness, and I have a large number of alumni out there for whom I have warm feelings. With all due respect to past and present employees, one of them stands out. Robert "Roger" Dorrington worked for/with my family and me for forty years. When I finally learned that he was—he would never say this—a war hero of the Greatest Generation, my respect for this man increased only marginally, because it always was high. Roger was awarded the Distinguished Flying Cross by Senator John McCain's grandfather. I have great admiration and affection for him, and I am proud and honored to have known him for over fifty-four years. His story as my favorite former employee deserves to be told.

I have had and, thankfully still have, so many wonderful clients over the years. Many of them are memorable, of course. One, who has passed, Bob Charpie, does stand out, and I have included a small segment about our relationship as well. He, also, was a man who commanded and deserved my respect and affection.

Baroness Pauline de Rothschild/Baron Philippe de Rothschild

One of the great women of wine passed away in 2014 at eighty years of age, Madame Philippine de Rothschild. She truly was a "Grande Dame de Bordeaux" and was an iconoclastic personage in the world of wine.

In years past I may have seen Philippine in passing at tastings, but never met her. I did, however, meet her illustrious father, Baron Philippe de Rothschild, at an intimate wine-tasting luncheon held at the Boston restaurant Pier Four in 1975. That meeting is indelibly imprinted in my mind. I have, somewhere in my office, a picture of the baron and me taken at the event. I look starstruck and intimidated, and indeed I was.

There were only eight or ten of us present at this tasting event, half of whom were representatives selling the Mouton Cadet brand, along with select classified châteaux. One of the reps, Harry, I forget his last name, went to the airport to get the baron, whose plane was late. There was a long table set up in a private room, and a place was left at the head of the table for Baron Philippe.

When the baron finally arrived, a Nehru suit adorning his five-foot-five-inch frame, his personal charisma was immediately evident as he took charge. "No, no, no!" he loudly exclaimed when he saw how the table was set up. "I want smaller tables in a semicircle around me, and I want a high chair to sit on."

Then the loudspeaker broke in, calling the numbers for diners who were waiting to be seated. That freaked the baron out. "That," he imperiously exclaimed with asperity, while pointing, "*must* be stopped *now*." Anthony Athanas, Pier Four's owner, who had his own imperious charisma, jumped up like a schoolboy to do the baron's bidding.

I don't remember the food or even what wine was served. I very well remember being mesmerized for an hour or two as Baron Philippe regaled us with stories about Mouton Rothschild, how he was the very first to château bottle his wine, and how he got famous artists to design his painted labels. He talked about his wife, Pauline, and about life in general. I was in awe of the man, an awe that has never left me.

In reading Philippine's obituary, I was struck initially by one thought. Did the opinionated, brilliant baron intend for Philippine to take over upon his death in 1988? Did she expect to do so; was she so groomed? Regardless of her pedigree, she was a woman in an extremely chauvinistic man's world. Although she was a lady, she had to be as tough as nails. But then, in thinking further about her background—losing her mother to the Nazis, nearly being sent to the camps herself, and living under the same roof as the famous, autocratic, temperamental baron—she had to have a resolve of iron and whip cord to survive and flourish.

There are increasing numbers of very successful women on both sides of the Atlantic who are involved in the wine world and have succeeded admirably. They are now too numerous to mention, but Anne Gros of Domaine Anne Gros in Vosne Romanee; May-Éliane de Lencquesaing, owner of Château Pichon Lalande; and Americans Helen Turley and Merry Edwards immediately come to mind. Philippine de Rothschild was one of the greatest of them all. Her loss will be felt around the world. May she rest in peace.

An Unsung Hero of the Greatest Generation

I have had some wonderful employees over the years and still do at present. One of my former employees stands out, and I would like to recognize him here. Despite our difference in age we were friends for over fifty years.

Tom Brokaw wrote in his 1998 book about World War II, *The Greatest Generation*, "It is, I believe, the greatest generation any society has ever produced." He argued that the men and women of that generation fought not for fame or recognition, but because it was the right thing to do. When they came back home, they rebuilt America into a superpower.

On Veteran's Day some years ago, I called my favorite former employee, Bob "Roger" Dorrington. Roger started work for my family in 1953 at the old store at 12–14 Massachusetts Avenue, Lexington, next to Mal's Towing. The store was located in front of the two family houses where my mom and dad had lived in the attic apartment when they were first married. Bob was thirty-three years old then and a World War II veteran. He never talked about his service in the navy but, prompted by an article in the *Boston Globe* regarding the dwindling population of the Greatest Generation, I began to subtly query him about it.

Before I tell you what he told me, I first would like to tell you about Roger, the man who worked with my family for forty years. When he started working for my uncle and dad at the (minuscule) old store, he was handsome, blond-haired, and blue-eyed. He was brought up in Arlington, Massachusetts, and lived on Whittemore Street, first with his parents and later in that same house with his beloved wife, Kay, and their six kids. Although he worked with us for forty years before retiring, that wasn't his main occupation. Roger was a captain and then acting deputy chief in the Arlington Fire Department. Roger may not have gone to college, but he was one of the most intelligent, pragmatic, capable people I have ever known. Working for my dad and uncle, who bickered constantly, had to be trying. I worked for them, too, but separately, and that was bad enough. Finally, when Roger had had his fill of their fighting he called them both aside. "Look," he said. "You guys don't get along, so why not use a fireman's shift. One of you could work Monday, Tuesday, Thursday. The other will work Wednesday, Friday, and Saturday. You can switch off anytime. We're only open from 9 a.m. to 9 p.m., and that will give you each multiple days off, and you won't get on each other's nerves." And that's what they did, for years, even after we moved the shop across the street in 1959 to the site of what was once the Newport Drive-In Restaurant.

Roger had/has a great sense of humor, and he and I loved to

talk of the old days and some of the funny episodes we both shared. Here's one. Early one morning, an elderly lady came into the shop, and Roger waited on her. When he gave her the change, she looked at the dollar bills and grimaced. She told him that one of the bills was "dirty." Roger took the bill back from her, looked at it, and, with a straight face, tossed it in the trash, gave her a fresh bill from the register, and said, "Thank you." If you could have seen the lady's expression as she looked from the trash to Roger's poker face and back again, you'd have cracked up, as did I. "Hey" he said, "if it's no good to you, it's no good to me." Of course, he fished it out after she left.

Did I say my dad and uncle were tough cookies to work for? We used to have a circular mirror at the corner of the beer chest. My dad liked to look in it to see if the "help" were working. One day he was peeking at the mirror, and Roger noticed. So he kept moving just a little bit further out of my dad's sight in the mirror, maneuvering him kind of like you'd get a turtle's head out of its shell. Finally, when my dad was all the way out of the office he said to Rog, "What the hell are you doing?" Roger said, "Hey, if you can see me, what makes you think I can't see you?"

Of course, his colleagues on the fire department knew where he worked part time. One time when Roger was on duty, he was called out on a run to assist a gentleman who was reported down on the sidewalk. The truck pulled up to assist the guy, and it was obvious that he was more than three sheets to the wind. When Roger and his men bent to help him, he looked up and with a beatific grin bellowed out, "Hey Roger! How ya doing?" One of the firemen said, "Boy, Roger, you sure do know all the important people."

On a more serious note: one day a fellow driving a Volkswagen Beetle raced into my parking lot, flew into the store, and asked to use the phone. Turns out that on Mass. Ave. across from the Village Food Store next to us, an eight- or ten-year-old kid had run into the street and was hit by a mail truck. I wasn't a trained paramedic, so I yelled downstairs to Roger and told him what had happened. I'll never forget him running full bore up those stairs, red of face, jowls flapping. He flew across the parking lot to try and help. Unfortunately, it was too late; the child died. The mail-truck driver was never the same and soon retired.

The Veteran's Day article in the *Globe* stated that one million Massachusetts men and women fought in World War II. Thirty-five thousand were still alive. The number is far less than that today. I got curious. Roger, with some gentle prodding, told me that he flew in a dive-bomber in the navy. He was assigned to the *Carrier Wasp*. Not the one destroyed earlier in the war, but *Wasp 2*. He was an aerial gunner in a Curtiss SB2C Helldiver, a two-seater, carrier-based plane. Looking it up online shows that it wasn't the safest or most reliable aircraft. God may well have been Roger's copilot, as he was twice rescued from planes that went down, once in the South Pacific and once in the Atlantic. On one mission, he told me, his squadron of twelve planes left the carrier for a mission against the Japanese at around four in the afternoon. "None of us had combat experience flying at night. Only one plane made it back to the ship. Eleven planes were lost, as were nine men. I was lucky," he said. "We were picked up the next day. But my pilot was killed on another mission."

Roger then asked me if he had ever told me that he was awarded the Distinguished Flying Cross. What? I since have learned that John McCain's grandfather, an admiral, was the presenter. Here's what I learned online: the Distinguished Flying Cross is a military decoration awarded to any officer or enlisted member of the United States Armed Forces who distinguishes himself or herself in support of operations by "heroism or extraordinary achievement while participating in an aerial flight, subsequent to November 11, 1918."

"Wow," I said. "No, you never did tell me." And this is a man I have known for fifty years. "How'd you get that?" I asked. "Well," he said, "I flew fifty-six missions." (Fifty-six missions! I get choked up just thinking about it.) "On the sixth mission there was a huge air battle against the Japanese. We lost a lot of men and planes. There was a Jewish kid from Brooklyn who I had become very friendly with in a plane just next to me. He was gone in a flash. I did a lot of damage to the Japanese that day," he recounted dryly. I left it at that.

Bob's daughter Anne, a nurse practitioner who had driven him to the shop that day, turned to me and said, "He has a lot of medals, but he doesn't like to talk about them."

I visited Roger several times the summer of 2017 while he was receiving Hospice care at the Bedford VA. He told me in a tone of wonder, "I never expected to live this long. I never had any serious accidents, and I never got sick." We did not talk about the war, only about funny incidents that happened at the shop. Before Roger passed away on Monday, July 17, 2017, he was mentally sharp to the end, and we had a lot of laughs together, like always, in spite of his weakened condition. On one visit, after I said goodbye and was out the door, heading down the hall, I heard Roger yell, "Joel!" I went back and said, "Yes, Rog?" He said, "You are going the wrong way. The elevators are that way." Swallowing a smile, I thanked him and headed in the right direction.

I'm glad I got to spend some time with him at the end. We shared an unbreakable bond of friendship that transcended age, religion, and circumstance. He was never "an employee" to me. Rather, he was a longtime family friend with whom I shared many memorable experiences. I will miss him, a lot.

Roger embodies all the great qualities exemplified in Brokow's book *The Greatest Generation*. He survived his beloved wife, Kay, who passed a few years back, and lived with his daughter Anne's family in Weston. Roger and his family are people who are the salt of the earth. He and they make me proud to be an American.

I have had and lost many wonderful customers over the years. I would like to mention one special customer now.

Bob Charpie

Bob Charpie also was a member of the Greatest Generation. During World War II, Dr. Charpie served in the Tenth Mountain Division of the United States Army, where he received two Bronze Stars for meritorious service.

I did business with Bob Charpie for well over thirty years. I always considered him to be the most aptly named person I have ever met. He was sharp, precise, and concise. Bob was introduced to me by one of my loyal customers who, like Bob, was a member of the Boston branch of the Wine and Food Society. He knew the passion for wine that we shared would be our common denominator despite our difference in age and position in life. At this time, Bob was chairman of Cabot Corporation. He had a personal charisma that, as the young people of today would say, was awesome. I know I regarded him with awe. Back then, I used to get my courage up before I would call him to tell him about a new offering that I knew he would most likely find appealing. This, of course, was well before the Internet. But even years after the advent of emails and online newsletters, I continued to communicate with him exclusively by phone. Invariably, his beloved wife, Beth, would call out, "Bob, Joel's on the phone."

After Bob answered, I would quickly tell him what I had to offer. He would rarely ask me any questions. He knew, and I knew he knew, the wine, the vintage, the grower, and what the price should be. His decision to buy or not usually was made in less than five seconds. He was either in or out that quickly and, either way, I ended the conversation just as quickly, with a "Thank you, Bob." Because I knew what wines he liked, at various price points from diverse areas, I was most fortunate to have him in far more often than out. Bob had great taste, with a crystal-clear vision of what would please him. When he moved he asked for my help transferring his cellar to his new home. I know that he was proud when I told him, "I have never seen so many across-the-board, diverse bottles of great wine in one place at one time."

Bob did call me a handful of times over the years, but this was not the norm. Interestingly, in all the years we did business together, he was only twice in my shop, even though I was only twenty minutes away. We always delivered the wine he ordered to his home. The second and last time I saw him at the shop was around five years ago, when he showed up unexpectedly with his son-in-law. The first time was well over twenty years ago, when I received a call from Bob. I believe it was on a Friday. I was very surprised when he said, "Will you be at the shop on Tuesday at one o'clock? Boston is the host city for the International Wine and Food Society in two years, and I want to discuss with you the wines we will need to order." I said, "Yes, sir. I'll be waiting."

At five minutes after one, Bob showed up, larger than life. We went into my modest office, and he gave me a list that had a breakdown of the type of wines he required, what regions they should be from, general price points, and expected quality levels. He wasn't more specific than that, as he trusted me to get him the best wines within the parameters dictated and, obviously, at the best price. Of course, I was honored and got right on it. As Bob knew, this is what I love to do, but certainly not usually on such a large scale. It was fun work for me, and after a week or so I was ready to report my findings and suggestions to Bob. Most of which he accepted, some he rejected. Some of the wines were on the cusp of acceptance for both of us, so we got samples and tried them.

In the end, he placed an extremely large order of mostly French wines, including Bordeaux, Burgundy, Champagne, and Rhône. Not all of them were household names, but all were of the highest provenance, pragmatically chosen by both of us for their quality and price. After we settled on the wines, Bob then said to me, for the first time, "We won't need these for nearly two years. Please cellar and store them for us." Really? It was tacit that no storage fees would be involved. When the event finally took place and the wines that we held were delivered, it became crystal clear how prescient Bob had been: those wines had increased in value by 50–100 percent.

Bob and his wonderful wife, Beth, have both passed away. He died three weeks after the love of his life. They were both most certainly extraordinary, one-of-a-kind individuals. He and Beth are missed by people other than the Charpie family. Both Bob and Beth were always so warm and gracious to my wife, Bonnie, and me. We were honored to be included at some of his great tastings over the years, including his great 1982 Bordeaux tasting, which also included '49s and '53s. I hope that they are both together, looking down with deserved pride at the family members who are carrying on their stead. The class, dignity, and humility exhibited by the entire Charpie family upon their passing was exemplary and impressive.

Final Thoughts

It is said that wine is a living thing. That doesn't mean it's going to jump up and chase you around the table. It means, with high-quality wines, there is change and development over a period of time. Wines from the same case will age and develop differently; each is unique, and that's part of the fun. We in the wine business say, "I had a great bottle of such and such." We individualize bottles of great wine because we know the next bottle will be different, maybe better, maybe not quite as good. What is sure: selling wine is a lot more fun than selling refrigerators.

There is so much to learn and know about wine that it is, or should be, refreshingly humbling. People often refer to me, or people like me, as "wine experts." I prefer to say that I am a "wine professional." I shun the "expert" tag. I like to tell a story about Frank Schoonmaker, a wine importer, retailer, and educator, the author of several very useful wine books. Legend has it that Mr. Schoonmaker was at a wine dinner one night when a middle-aged lady cornered him and said, "You're Mr. Schoonmaker, the man who knows everything about wine." He looked at her and replied, "Madame, if that were true today, it wouldn't be true tomorrow." I am in no way comparing my wine knowledge to Frank's, but I feel the same way. There is so much to know that it would be impossible for one person to grasp it all. And that's good. Therefore there are no "stupid" questions that one might ask about wine. If any wine person answers a question with an attitude or with condescension, they should quit the trade and go do something else.

I have been fortunate to have my avocation be my vocation. I work with highly intelligent people on all levels of the wine business: producers, purveyors, growers, staff, and clients. Although it takes some effort to find interesting, fun, and affordable wines, from wherever, I love doing just that. I love the wine business and still look forward to what the new day may bring. I have no interest in quitting anytime soon, if ever.

Let me say: I am sure that there will be some who read sections of this book and disagree with some of my observations. That's OK and to be expected. I have tried to be as accurate in my statements as I can, but it is possible that there may be some facts in dispute, no matter how careful I have been. I hope not, but am not naïve. There may be some things in the book that someone may take exception to or be offended by. Again, I hope not, but anything is possible. If I have made any inadvertent errors or have offended anyone in any way, let me say that was not my intent and, if so, I am sorry.

CPSIA information can be obtained
at www.ICGtesting.com
Printed in the USA
BVHW03s2027090418
512936BV00002B/4/P

9 781627 875875